GW01312806

Jesus Reimagined
in shared moods and emotions

Phil Streeter

ACKNOWLEDGEMENTS

My appreciation to Tony Collins for his early guidance, to Bridget Boyle for her proof reading and to John Thackray for rescuing me from my many computer problems. Also Patrick Gaughan for his pleasing cover design and a galaxy of other inspired people who have dropped small, priceless thoughts into my contemplative lap and that are now embedded in the structure of this book.

"The life, thoughts, deeds, aims, beliefs of Jesus have to be fresh expounded every age, for all the depth of eternity lies in them, and they have to be seen into more profoundly every new era of the world's spiritual history."
(George MacDonald)

"The snake which cannot cast its skin has to die. As well the minds which are prevented from changing their opinions; they cease to be mind."
(Friedrich Nietzsche)

CONTENTS

	Page
Introduction.	1
Earthiness.	5
Weakness.	13
Playfulness.	25
Femininity.	41
Sensuality.	49
Foolishness.	65
Anger.	70
Sexuality.	79
Madness.	89
Doubt.	98
Epilogue	110

INTRODUCTION

More poet less theologian, I'm exaggerating, playing 'make believe' and speculating like someone on a blind date; reading into things and doctoring statements to concoct romance, but no more than those who twist biblical statements into hard dogma and fierce rules. My theme concerns Jesus *the man*, not unlike us but with something added; an historical figure who cannot be 'solved.' The more I think I understand him, greater the shock if I happened to meet him, his originality not dependent on textual expositions.

Guessing at his moods and emotions while never intending to be correct, I resort to hyperbole, 'perhaps' and 'maybe,' Seneca suggesting that hyperbole must lie to hint at truth. While my descriptions might be wrong, they could also be fragments of some ridiculous reality prompting interpretation of possible emotions in the light of my own.

Semitic in personality, emotional in temperament, Jesus was undoubtedly effusive and animated. A man of many temperaments, emotions and vivid imagination. Kidnapped by religious solemnity, forced to carry doctrinal baggage and interpreted from insufficient information, he needs rescuing from time, logic and literalism.

Misinterpreted by intimations of impeccable behaviour in developing the Conductor we have disfigured the Composer. Difficult to understand due to limited information, misleading literalism and editorial meddling, the account we have of his life is not a definitive one. Thinking, speaking considerably more than is recorded, laws and standards have been added making him in need of de-cluttering from ideologies and pious moralists. For this reason, I make feeble attempts to step beyond his Jewishness and Christian-ness. Unable to delve into his head, I must resort to conjecture, removing him from the Bible without the Bible expelled from him, the most tantalising being all that's left out. Crossing borders between fact and fiction, eschewing jargon and inflexible thinking, I picture him as I imagine him to be then and now.

More astonishment than dull example, Jesus never set out to create doctrine and establish a new religion, in fact, much of his teaching appears secret, ambivalent, and not intended for public hearing. He simply wished people to see, feel and enjoy surrounding wonders. To ask themselves questions of life, death, time and eternity. To sense exciting mysteries of existence, explore felt depths, embrace beauty and respectfully care for one another – that's all!

Desiring to see and hear him speak, I must think of aspects that are missing, imagining nuances of mood and visualising all I cannot see. When a historical person cannot be seen, one must explore the imagination. The earthy Jesus must be envisaged rather than literalised, for anything that can be imagined, exists. To approach truth is not via literalism but jumps of imagination. Imagination is a fragment of God's image in us. It must be *felt* – a marvelling at something we feel to be grander than any stated text. Painting a wall, one first imagines a colour, I therefore romanticise rather than literalise, earnestly hoping I'm inventing situations that may have happened.

No evil in guessing, I resort to hyperbole not exactness. To fancifully wonder, whimsically speculate, apply make-believe, flirt with reason rather than law and tell fibs for the glory of God, only then can I hope to capture images hindering or helpful depending on the reader. As Rumi said, "A tale fictitious or otherwise, illuminates truth." Maybe inaccuracies offer a truer overall picture than literal exposition – nothing like I describe but still real. If earliest artists invented Jesus from scratch, I too must re-touch paintings in search for an impressive person.

The irony of exaggerated reasoning is that it easily becomes personal conviction. As someone said, to read him right, Jesus must be spelt wrong, a difference existing in the life he lived as well as the life the Bible presents to us. Open to limitless definitions he adjusts to contemporary interpretations. Filling in gaps of all we don't know and reading between the lines, he becomes what he's meant to be to **each individual**.

Without pressing for structured neatness, I think Jesus followed instinct and feeling, the potency of his words oozing out of emotional awareness in contrast to unshakeable apostolic interpretation. Many meanings are lost because we have no conception of an entirety of which they are bits and pieces. Bible statements in themselves, like any book, are frozen voices until translation into imagined images. There's a thrill in imagining events that might or might not have happened, imagination being the greatest means to understanding. To imagine is to discover. "Knowledge is limited," said Einstein "whereas imagination embraces the entire world." Reading is imagining. Searching people feed their imagination, in doing so, they become artists and poets, fools and heretics.

Recalling Virginia Woolf's opinion that "Any method is right, every method is right that expresses what we wish to express," Being "*Poet made flesh,"* I think his limited life is best captured in inseparable prose/poetry forms rather than theological accuracy, be it like my own disordered free-verse and unstructured prose reflecting my faith and feelings. Not wanting to isolate poetry from prose, I experiment with a disorderly inventiveness in the style of French poets Charles Peguy and Michel Quiost. Ignoring rules for the ease of breaking them, poetic sentiments become means of writing prose or is it the other way round? Extravagant evocations rather than literal meanings, more pictures than historical records prompting A .E. Housman to insist that poetry not having to be genuine truth, is an emotional process where the heart always rules the head. For this reason, I sometimes put *my own* words into the mouth of Jesus. While not inspired facts, they at least point to possible reality outside of written history, to an elusive figure open to re-interpretation in every generation.

I would add that some Bible books were written in poetic forms and meant to be read aloud just as human lives are. Jesus was poet not theologian, his words, more poetry than dogma, encouraged listeners to explore who they were. To flop his poetry is to miss his message. Deepest, most sacred encounters in my life have visited me in poetic shapes not theoretical teaching. If I slip into sentimentality, I've no regrets; it's a poet's perk!

I would briefly and apologetically remark that in linking many thoughts, outside material may have accidently been included without acknowledgement. For these lapses I plead forgiveness. I haven't referenced Bible texts cruelly abandoning readers to sort them out for themselves if they so wish.

PHIL STREETER.

EARTHINESS

The first thing is to know Jesus as a man, and any theory about him that makes less of him as a man – with the foolish notion of exalting his divinity I refuse at once.
George MacDonald (letter to his father)

Christian detachment is still too often advocated or understood as an attitude of indifference, suspicion or contempt towards the realities of the earth. The world we know is but dust and slime, and "the less contact we have with it the saintlier we shall be" … in itself, contact with matter most certainly does not defile the soul or drag it down: on the contrary, it feeds the soul and elevates it.
Teiilhard de Chardin

A person walks upright and the food in their body is shut in as if in a well-made purse. When the time of their need arrives, the purse is opened and then shut again in most fitting fashion. And it is God who does this, as it is shown when he says that he comes to us in our humblest needs. For God does not despise what he has made, nor does he disdain to serve us in the simplest natural functions of our body, for the love of the soul which he created in his own likeness.
Julian of Norwich

He became like me, in order that I might accept him: in appearance he seemed like me, in order that I might put him on… He became like my nature in order that I might learn to know him, and like my form in order that I might not turn away from him.
**Odes of Solomon
(early gnostic gospel)**

They named him, adding the preliminary politeness, endorsing a claim to gentility he did not possess.
R. S. Thomas

EARTHINESS

Material or spiritual,
    Sacred or secular.
    Human or divine.
Partitions gossamer thin – where does one end and another begin?
Deeper the plunge into religious fervour, more loss of reality,
Piety and blessedness our silliest faux pas, worshipping baby innocence, ignoring fetid feet.
Purity purging barbarity, earliest Saints and Seers doused in stricken soil not holy water, sour sweat instead of hallowed light, their solemn thoughts wrestling with slummy vulgarity, their holy bones chewed to dust.

WORMS AND CHERUBIMS

Weakest of weak wade altar-deep through steaming sacrifices, evaporated beliefs, miserable joy and mental disintegration.
Helplessly resisting, they survive gravelly days and toothy nights, the bloodiness of life and dizzy seizure of death.
In blessings and curses, ecstasies and guilt, supernatural clumsiness and yokel idiocy, their every hope greater than realised.

In galleries grotesque, Noah exposes himself in drunken nudity.
    Abraham and family indulge in lies and deception.
    Samson lip-licks in sexual stalk and pounce.
    Elijah – intolerant showman, cracks lavatory jokes.
    David, terrible in sins, lyrical in poetry, squirms in syphilitic agony.
    Ezekiel guzzles excrement and men everywhere make solemn oaths clutching one another's testicles. 1.
Grubby and repugnant, hidden Hydes embody cackling Jekylls damaged in mind, stunted in sainthood –
Crippling encumbrances masking intensities of innocence as gritty *God* chokes scummy man with earthy incense.
"My covenant shall be in your flesh" – *God* mixed with passionate earth in veiled purity.
Creator stooping to creature in mud, brothels and massage parlours amid earth's dark respectability.
One and All grubbing among tortured clay, higher than humanness yet shaped by it.
Filthiness copulating with beauty, opulence with squalor, awakening soil manures history for coming *Earthy One*.

ARRIVAL IN RECOGNISABLE SHAPES

Devoid of majesty, in God he's small, in man he's great.
Intruding into life, he tumbles to ground below to see sky above.
No book or building, but *"Poem made flesh,"* talking, laughing, despairing and other

incomprehensible moods and idiosyncrasies like our own:
"*That which we have looked upon and our **hands have handled**"* – human flesh
announcing the wonder of God spirituality linked to body sensuality, the
unusual erupting among the commonplace in home-made roughness.
More friend than deity, a tired man carved into images of who we are, for only in
earthiness is reality realised – our humanness ever equal with his.
No flamboyance or detachment from the material, but enlightened unpretentious
stranger in soiled sandals; infinity's clod of life spattered with the soil of his day.
"*Born of a woman,*" human smiles, human teeth, human genitals, speaking our
language in familiar acts and words – "*made like his brothers in every way,*"
insisting on anything different makes him freakish.
Clothes soured with sweat, flesh reeking of fatigue, springing from earth, how can he
not smell of it?
Son of earth in common form, highest DNA embedded in grimy hands and probing eyes
fixed earthward, the lark touching ground before rising to the sky.
No heavenly idealism or self-conscious decorum but humanness anchored in mystery,
transcendence in simplicity, infinity in mundanity,
So where's the border between divinity and humanity?
Uncanny burying itself in humanness transforms it making him like everyone, meeting
him like meeting someone else, physical and more than physical mingling,
matter, and spirit never at odds.
Little formality, casual but never intrusive, diversity swims through blood and body, a
man of gritty amiability, animal delight, elation and depression, messy and
sublime but everything holy, simple and obvious.
Greatest Achievement dragged from isolation, tools left cluttered on a carpenter's
bench, few scruples in eating, drinking and give-and-take conversation, he
never imagines other than who he is.
No demands to be honoured and worshipped, but peering through dirt he escapes
prayers sermons and pietistic paintings.

EARTHY AND UNCOMFORTABLE

One'd with earth in pleasure and profanity, not hiding decency but unaware of it,
astonishment enters familiarity, the divinity of man alive in circumstance and
activity, inwardness balancing outward-ness, each routine catching breath with
eternal meanings.
Normal but never dull, signatures of sanctity in dirty feet and sunburnt face, he's son of
soil and man of familiar looks among hollered oaths, bad teeth, smelly breath
and chipped fingernails – a lyrical fallibility and graspable oddity without loss of
strangeness.
A self-oblivious spiritualty, emotionally life-like rather than obscurely foreign, resembling
us more than we him, if not, how could he be approached?

Refinement in earthiness, suspiciously special,
Like *Aslan*, he must be touched, stroked, smelt and patted,

true religion never absent of feel and smell in beating blood and squeeze of warm flesh.

Rough-hewn from personal experience, void of finesse with earth-born interest in people because they're there, he's scent of silt in common sense.

Identified with tent, stable and criminal crucifixion, a shabby depiction of cordiality, routine and mulch of rough and ready flesh – flowers bursting into colour when rooted in sticky soil.

Meaningless without manhood, pragmatism saturates reverence, dishevelment polishes reality and spirituality absorbs material or not at all.

Red-blooded, un-ambitious for perfection, salt of reality confronting treacly sentimentality, he's swathed in humdrum, dust billowing around calloused feet, halo dropped liked trousers round his ankles.

Borrowed humanity smirched in leaden dirt and ineffable dust, grimy body smells infuse crumpled folds, his bitter breath consecrated in familiar talk and body experience.

Outdoor odours drench him in generous lumps, confused streets and straggle of puzzled people.

Facets of life meaningful, nothing human failing fulfilment and truth never perfected until fused with mortality.

No preachiness and chilly isolation, weepy music or heavenly glances, but in dunginess identifying with earthy surroundings he's happier in inns where fools carouse than temples shrouded in mysticism, easy with mud beneath his feet more than heaven above his head.

Void of aloofness, touchable grandeur spills into mood and fancy, the holiness of the mundane, a purity promenading with material, ascension downwards appearing in highest things rarely found together and commonplace rousing noisy cheers majestic as concert and celebration.

SCHOLAR OF THE SOIL

An organic spirituality – *Scholar of Soil* alchemising squalor and sublimity, struggle and astonishment, sickness and disintegration.

No far-off hermit from Galilean hills but man of dreary radiance in earthy similitudes of where we exist, slipping in excrement of human uselessness and dredging rawness out of respectability.

In every way like us, no part untouched by deity in shifty stench and volatile passions, matter-of-fact fatigue and dumped garbage of desires not understood, our very dust having ancestry of splendour surpassing anything seen and felt.

No coy, prettified Christ but complex and contradictory, *"As he is, so are we in this world."*

Sharing flesh and common vulnerability, speaking body things without shame he ascends to animal man in weary tension, scruffy shape and roughest manners.

The unsurprisingly strange, the physical sacramental, his every routine an *"instant elsewhere."* 2.

Wrapped in rags, conceived in calcium, *"he's with us,"* jotted Blake, *"because he did not abhor the uterus."*
No tapestry of luminous beings or glistening lights but *"dear little rags."*
Earthiness in stale urine and severed foreskin, sodden straw, and rancid animal breath.
Void of cute soaps reeking of roses, dirty nappies drape among donkey droppings, sour bodies and a *"carnal cradle,"* railed poet Peguy.
Flustered flies, watching spiders and screams of baby irritability litter his fearful world.
An earthy danger too hot to tread on, a chaotic below-ness from wriggling child to nailed victim.

MAJESTY OF THE ORDINARY

Self-titled *Son of Man* signals nothing mysterious but familiarity as few know it.
Creator's birth mark, flawless in form, impossible in attraction, wretched in weakness, footprints of immanence dent a vagabond world in stench and splendour.
Delivered from dogmatics, an answerless conundrum, a disturbed intruder.
In reverential crudeness, man of familiar talk doing undignified things:
> chin-wiping after sucking a bone,
> brazen in peeing and vomiting,
> blood and spittle,
> grunting and breaking wind,
> talking in his sleep,
> vomiting and defecating in rippled sand –

Physical, poetic responses de-mystifying Bible, church, priesthood and no less sacred than Eucharist, Mass or Holy Communion.
In stinking sweat and ugly swellings, estrangement and mood change, insect bite and unwashed skin, every normality making unmentionables mentionable in coughing, sneezing, hiccupping and grinding teeth.
Eternity crashing into time in indigestion and disease,
> diarrhoea and headaches, hot sweats and cold fevers,
> sapping nausea, runny nose and
> rugged celebration of libidinal desires.

No dentist, doctor, chiropodist or therapist and like ourselves, easy victim to Covid that uninvited guest, an 'important' apostle insisting *"Those parts of the body that seem weaker are indispensable, and the parts we think less honourable* **… treat with special honour."**

Heights demanding depths make him more human than humans, boundaries paper thin between divinity and humanity.
Refusing to be pinned down, domesticated by health and safety, protected by political correctness or converted to dignified doctrine, he's highest among the vulgar and absentee from Christian clubs.
Grabbing dirt and disorder, smirched with dust and sand, no boasted prudery in himself, physical and spiritual couple in common phlegm and raging illness, toothache, constipation and contagious disease – even holy mystics and sun-tanned

models visiting toilets, an everyday event in his age, puppy sanitised tissue in our own.
But why etiquette if there's no enthusiasm or honesty sacrificed for respectability?

SMUG EXCEPTIONALISM

Emptied of religious poise, kidnapped by polite sermons, behaviour at church and dinner table prudery makes him unimaginable!
Shocking conventional respectability, would he recognise himself among tidy texts and protected dogma, born-again niceness and boring games of respectability, wrinkled noses and foppish reverence mortified at all it sees, hears and smells.
Scented sprays fighting losing battles with soiled clothes, body odour and inspired disarray.
Smug concern and primness over stained clothes, eating with fingers and snobbish habits interfering with well-ordered worlds, making theological debate about him senseless.
"The sparrow has found a home, and the swallow a nest for herself where she may have her young – a place near your altar, O Lord Almighty."
Evidently, *Deity's* not bothered about bird droppings!

Viewed against Kleenex convictions, challenging good taste and convention, rinsed, ironed and made middle-class by god-fearing cleanliness, he's been adorned and crowned by busy-body saints, muzzled, fettered and restricted like helpless Gulliver.
The founder of an *"incurably irreverent religion,"* 3. thrust outside bathrooms, displaced from kitchen realism, for more fervent the plunge into religion, greater the loss of human normality.
Spirituality has fallen into the hands of the respectable with its religiously eau-de-cologned demands in order to smother the smells.
Manicured and sentimentalised in prayer and praise, the *Intruder,* disembodied into unreality disrupts ordered beliefs and tidy altars, doctrinal literalism a pane of glass separating uniformed man of Sunday dignity reduced to controllable proportions.
Anarchical energies tamed, earthy spirituality diluted and downgraded by decorative devotion, ceremony and ritual, *Son of Man* is cribbed into Christianity.

Would he recognise himself in follower's portrayals, never spotting him in profanity as well as purity, flesh as well as faith?
Why solemnity in a life that doesn't need it and is best without it?
Incarnated anywhere finds him there already, hiding beneath structure and symbolism, questioning thought and pagan appearances, earthy informality his seamless robe – finding loose strands and unravelling someone clasping contradictory ideas in harmony.
As he is, we are, familiar as yesterday in essence of ordinariness, love for *God* no different from love for people and none of us more holy by making ourselves less human.

A holy earth of brushing teeth and distressing hygiene, doubting, lusting and other renegade adventures alien to angels.
A salvation of untidiness, a discovery of who we are, not who we become – one with Deity germinating humus of soiled bodies in slip of the tongue, forgetfulness and multi-wrapped emotions – settled mud making the reservoir clear.

COMFORTABLE WITH DISCOMFORT

I cannot carve elegance into butterflies or resist deepening blue of twilight, only able to distort, his life challenges my prejudices, faces me with my ignorance while persuading me to remain human.
A holiness in earthiness not dejection in fallenness, patient with my contradictions, ignoring all that Christians expect of me, only believing what I understand and possessing little faith if any in the religious sense of the word.
Given freedom to sin and fail, my many violations become awareness of my needs, my crimes redemptive aids not demoralising impediments – everything a gravelly biography of myself knotted to my owner.
'Materialist,' 'humanist,' supposedly Christian, not as good as *God* but as good as me, improved upon but never perfected, a never satisfied finder, worse than people think but better for my mistakes, not fighting failings but letting them be for cutting back the nettles only increases their growth.
Aware of all-embracing human failings, with Tertullian, *"I believe because it's impossible."*

1. A solemn practise in Old Testament times.
2. Andrew Graham Dixon.
3. Warner Allen.

WEAKNESS

*Jesus will overcome you, cried the minister (God the Wrestler).
Jesus will have his way with you (God the Rapist).
Jesus is going from strength to strength (God the Body Builder).*
Jeanette Winterson

*It is easy to die for something forceful because participation in force
produces an intoxication which stupefies us. But it is supernatural to
die for something weak: thousands of men were able to die heroically
for Napoleon, whilst Christ in his agony was deserted by his disciples.*
Gustave Thibon

*I prefer to fail having known the beauty of flowers than to
triumph in the wilderness, for triumph is the blindness of
the soul left alone with its own worthlessness.*
Jeanette Winterson

*Winning does not tempt that man. This is how he grows; by being defeated
decisively by constantly greater things.*
Rainer Maria Rilke

*The basic element I admire in Christianity is its sense of moral failure.
That is its very foundation.*
Graham Greene

*No vital force comes into the figure unless a man breathes into it all the hate
or all the love of which he is capable. The stronger the love, or the stronger
the hate, the more life-like is the figure which is produced. For hate as well
as love can write a life of Jesus and the greatest of them are written with hate.*
Albert Schweitzer

WEAKNESS

Like ourselves, entering life helpless and unobtrusive,
he's restrained existence in restricted time and
eternity adjusted to minutes.
Small in immensity, winning by submission, an undersized figure huge with history, a
profound loser stamped with failure.
No swarthy Commander of swaggering toughness, battle-hardened hero or charismatic
leader but humility that never grovelled,
unassuming servant towel draped over the arm,
impressive statue imprisoned in marble waiting to be damaged and made
beautiful.

Absence of arrogance to be other than who he is, void of moral pomposity and celebrity
gloss, contented in defeat he strolls among many while remaining alone.
Never considering himself original, a wanderer in pleasing strangeness his ordinariness
containing strength, his innocence void of naivety.
Born to unwed parents, has he entered Earth by mistake, minuteness denying
humanness until tiny mother nods consent?
Manger baby, six days old, wrinkled fingers, dewdrop toes, drop the ornament and it
shatters.
Flimsy child, awkward and demanding in boyhood, nobody born wise, all having to
attain it.
Small among childhood routine, it's time to pack bags and run for protection!

AGONY OF THE UNFORSEEN

Prophet of doubt speaking nonsense making sense, *"Is not this Joseph's son?"*
A bare-headed figure on a hill, passer-by giving suffering a human face, abstract artist
who can't be understood, his inspiration ending in failure.
No fighter geared to performance or trendy leader promising success, for many, a
passing hiccup in textbooks of time.
Earnestly defenceless, discriminated by his accent, aware of his limitations, shuffling
more than galloping, he limps toward people unprepared for him.
Never asserting his rights, no reluctance to express emotions,
Virtues of weakness and energies of helplessness are embraced,
vulnerability making deepest connections,
secret agonies at odds with public appearances and
headlong recklessness resulting in grim self-sacrifice.
In contrast to victorious God claimed as ally by the strong, his vulnerability an attraction,
his fragility strength.

*"Can any good **thing** come out of Nazareth?"*
"Does he think we're fools?"

Denying his influence, authority is acknowledged, possessing charm people fight battles because of it.
Servant not leader, child among adults hoping to be taken seriously, he's *nearly* successful in giving all he can – wanting nothing, receiving nothing in dignity and composure:
No honouring applause or confetti of praise but grinding years mending furniture.
With little admiration, disqualified by the pious, misunderstood by friends, reprimanded by family and vandalised by enemies, he's part of the people but not quite!
A perilous person dressed like everyone, looking like everyone, never intruding into their lives, sympathetic with their weaknesses his kindness is absent of interference.
Opposite to the expected, a footnote shuffling into history, a hesitation dropped into time, a simplicity challenging certainty, a *"reed shaken by the wind."*
"Is not this the carpenter's son?" the here-and-now, matter of fact and awkwardly out of place?
The *"Something almost being said,"* 1. starved of compliments, emptied of recognition, self-deprecating and surprised.
A character in an unfinished play, poet-in-chains, chapter in a rarely read book, a dog-eared scrap of paper inscribed with weighty words.
Would we pass him at a bus stop or ignore him on a crowded train?
Sadly, a heretics life is a lonely one.

POWER RESTS IN NOT HAVING TO PROCLAIM IT

Unsure how things will end, his unselfishness condemned and renounced, he epitomises positives of helpless acceptance, teetering uncertainty and faltering confidence,
Losers more truthful than winners, failures more interesting than successes and humble resignation the unique attribute of victims.
Void of competitive instinct, ignoring empty-sounding success, never bragging about miracles and dismissing hero worship, he grizzles: *"Why do you call me good?"*
Does he know himself, transcendence a frightful burden to bear?
Straddling two worlds, did he question who he was and where he belonged?
No eminence for self-preservation – prey more than gladiator, slitting wrists of reputation, dignity drains away – a Matterhorn squashed in a matchbox, a reservoir drained into a teacup.
Paradox of feebleness, noble in melancholy, fame is shunned for faintness, conquest for vulnerability, performance for hiddenness.

PROGRESS BY RETREATING

Deepest natures are victims to despondency.
Suspicions of his origins, recognition and respect withdrawn, he's alone among confused thoughts.
Besieged by doubts, playing the incompetent, he surely muttered sensible banalities, disillusionment depicting states of mind.
White-knuckled spirituality brushed aside:

> "I feel weary this morning."
> "Another futile day."
> "Is it worth the stress?"
> "Ouch, this damn headache!" and other feelings impossibly tedious – or else, feelings hidden, he pretends!

Unaware of what will happen tomorrow, like ourselves, long days and dragging moments, eager intentions but frustration in realising them.
Thirty years and the path leads too far, the effort demanding, the end too distant, a vision struggling to appear – speculation and supposition making reality bearable.
Is he seeking deeper identity?
Should he return to the carpenter's shop?
Was he furious with his helplessness?
Must he rack his brain, create strategies or keep pushing boulders uphill until they roll back on top of him?
Extraordinarily forceful in public, he hides composure in private.
Plaything of the repetitive, fumbling through the obvious, his stupefied feelings difficult to grasp by dreamers of deities who don't appear like people.
No mountainous doctrine, oceans of advice or warnings booming out of darkness, but unaware, he beguiles with nimble words, haunts with unintentional looks, convinces by home-spun normality and in passive non-leadership, leads!

No wickedly wearisome *"Thou shalt nots."*
> *"You must believe this!"*

Stronger the leader, greater the paranoia – power best appearing in not showing it.
Idling for anonymity, he's *Nearly Nothing*, non-threatening, non-manipulative, no strident certainties demanding obedience, just, *"Give to Caesar what belongs to him."*
He did and was left with nothing!
Never ravenous for recognition, the stray dog wanders dismal streets:
A shooting star nobody wishes on, a child's tooth ignored by fairies.
Always asking questions out loud, a shuffler muttering self-deprecating words as flat as crushed stones: *"If it be possible …"*
> *"Why do you call me good?"*
> *"Who touched me?"*
> *"I can of myself do nothing."*
> *"Save me from this hour."*
> *"Take this cup from me."*
> *"My God, where are you?"* – always the imaginative attacked by doubts.

Unconscious of goodness as primroses their perfume, a reed bending to the wind, doubt contradicts authority.
Maybe he's disenchanted idealist, carrying what can't be understood, questioning his potential, name on the cover yet uncertain of the contents?
> In broken bits of self-approach never begging applause, ordinariness makes him monumental.

SELDOM-NESS OF UNDERSTANDING

Shadowed by ambivalence, burdens are born that can't be laid down.
Aware of limitations, dismissing grandness, he stutters, *"No one's good except God."*
Pressed for opinions, answers are refused.
Challenged with questions, response is, *"What do **you** think?"*
Longing to be understood, a bewildered figure rejected and impeded.
A blind man feeling with a stick, puzzled about *God,* people and like poet Rilke,
    choosing to remain *"perpetual beginner."*
In sheepish curiosity and humble self-scrutiny, *"Who do people say I am?"* as if stopping
    in the street pleading directions to forgotten places.
Is he begging compliments or bait casting to sound out opinions?

Dithering, he enquires: *"I'm unsure what I'm doing."*
    "My time has not yet come."
Easily disturbed, quietly grappling with exclusion and despondency, the doe shivers on
    the edge of the forest, the buttercup bends under the weight of bees.
Tying his own hands, he gives what he doesn't have in meaningful failure.
But why no explanations on problems of pain, peppered light on the meaning of evil,
    consoling glimpses into after-life unknowns?
Was he aware that he'd be the cause of martyrdom and suffering, answered prayers
    begged for rarely given and God grinning at our selfish secret schemes?

Small in his world, gallant weakness lobs sceptres aside to pick lilies, beauty residing in
    smallness, attraction in detail.
How can greatness touch littleness without diminishing itself?
Often, right choices are not to succeed, a mumbled, "I failed," substance of successes.
What we term 'wrong,' frequently becomes right, and matters found comfortable to
    believe frequently false,
Religion over-impressed by greatness – great leaders, great faith, great miracles, but
    bulk quickly loses power to increase, smallness and least-ness lingering long
    after greatness has gone.

Banned as outlaw, victim to heresy-hunters, crushed by indifference and striving to build
    on religious ruins, he fails.
    Destiny doubted, closest friends – the passionate few, question his intentions,
    one foul mouths, another double-crosses and all desert him as plots play out in
    betrayal and execution.
Never impetuous, he's clouded by troubles that haven't happened and concerned about
    losing what he's never had.
Ducking from sight, fleeing his enemies, hunted down as troublemaker, it takes a hero
    to become a heretic.
More the retreat, greater the advance, meanwhile, *"many turned back from following
    Jesus,"* crowds dissolving leaving him nowhere to go.
Keeping respectable distances didn't he sensibly say: *"When they persecute you in one
    city, **flee** to another,"* frequently, escape is more torturous than resistance.

Running dangers of scorn, the hedgehog curls into a ball, the snail retreats into its shell.
    *"They picked up stones to throw at him but Jesus **hid himself**."*
Against hopeless odds, folly becomes heroic.
If fleeing is weakness among hatred and violence, honest doubt is commendable!
Rather than reeking vengeance or parading bravery, he dashes off, gameplay lines
    between prudence and cowardice, caution and outwitting, razor thin.
Can humiliation turn to humorous gentleness and how much heroism is expected of a
    person?
"Sometimes the opposite of cowardice is playfulness," suggested George Sand –
    ringing a neighbour's doorbell and running away!
A sideways glance, the licking of a finger and holding it to the wind, no hollow bravado
    but semi-anxiety or unbearable vulnerability.
Amused, maybe he's playing the doltish, misleading his friends as well as his enemies.
A 'spiritual dodge,' a serene self-contradiction, making compromise possible without
    losing ideals.
Sometimes, to do right, wrongs must be done, later actions bearing no resemblance to
    confident earlier statements.
Truth in disguise, courageous in cowardice, he's *"wise as serpents,"* fleeing in faith and
    throwing caution in the air to see what happens.
Like ourselves, sensible precautions, an Arabian proverb insisting, *"The highest level of
    courage is running away."*
Reserve and shyness, will and purpose that isn't cowardice any more than refusing sex
    in public would be.

Higher the being, smaller its revealed power, splendours of a stream at its estuary not
    its source.
Ill-prepared and unsure, he stays close to those who don't desert him –
    victim of fury thriving on being written off,
    hunted animal snuffing air through widening nostrils,
    agonised supplicant beneath slivered moon in a twilight garden.
Abandoned by intimacies held dear, longing for comfort, yearning for reliability, he clings
    to people like vines to trellises, seaweed to sunken ships.
Consequences inevitable, like pantomime children we yell, *"Look out! Someone's
    behind you!"*
But drained, subdued, like Alice swimming in her tears, *"Jesus wept."*
Sensing life's superficiality, follies of infallibility and triumph craftily imposed, he shrinks
    from emboldening himself.
Desperate for security it's denied him, dismissing his mother he needs her.
Tottering on life's abyss, gripped by unknowns, he's confusion and aloneness, rejection
    and betrayal, countless expectations with no fulfilments.
Like ourselves, creeping dread and runaway doubt with sporadic flashes of
    understanding.
Better this than delusions of grandeur and self-satisfied faith.
Despised as idiot, feared as examiner, a descent into limitation.
Shuddering under starlight he loses power, physical weakness never beautiful.

BEARING THE UNBEARABLE

Spurned and spat out, he fears.
Baleful clouds writhing in tortured thoughts, thread-thin humanity plummets into distress.
In a world loathing feebleness, stupidity revels in failure and up to no good he's lobbed onto garbage heaps then blamed for being there, the most conspicuous the most hated, the outsider most abused.
Object of fun, his image is inflated in efforts to destroy it, when gone, religion will feel safer.
Mouthing opposites he must be silenced, allowing himself to become expendable, he becomes expendable.
Groping within he hauls up emptiness, every word blitzed by misunderstanding.
No *Eternal* nose pressed against shuttered windows, no sympathising *Deity* weeping behind closed curtains – tricked by history, the nightingale laments.
Why struggle when stakes are hopeless?
Baffled and horrified, body breakable, power seized, he slumps into divine absence.
But solace excels in emptiness – emptiness impossible to share.
Plans, interests, happiness and dreams – yes, emptiness never.
Croaking nothing, a distant shore sinks into the horizon, the briefest gust of perfume, the undistinguished identified by a kiss.
Drawing straws he loses, speechless, no defence is offered.
Head bent toward his inferiors, the offended initiates the healing.
Courteous before Judas biting the hand that feeds him, silence before Herod, the cat contemplating friendship with the mouse, attentive before Caiaphas, respectful toward panic-stricken Pilate terror is tempered by defiance ...
"Father, forgive them, they don't know what they're doing."
Caged in custody, incarcerated by ignorance, skin thick enough to endure is thin enough to feel.
A swaying body needs help to carry its cross, stumbling, extended hands grab thin air, brokenness sinks into nothingness – spectacular weakness becoming *"the power and wisdom of God."*
Honoured by his own extermination, truth mixes with lies:
"He saved others but can't save himself!"
"Your God has abandoned you!"
"Give us Barabbas!"
"Curse him! He's a heretic."
Infuriated by his weakness, the *Different* must be suppressed.
Pelted with hisses and curses, nodding, smirking, winking, ferocious voices lavish significance; a poetic birth, a criminal's death, *"Mind bolder, heart braver, courage greater as strength grows less."* 2.

Wisdom resides in defeat not victory.
Commitment to things loved, demands a wasting away, a loss without losing, an awareness of life given not grabbed, truest triumph squirming from private failure.

Whatever reduces strengthens, to produce fruit, blossoms fade and fall, entering Wonderland one must become small.
Whiffs of exultation in desperate failure, tragedy crouching in nobility, dignity in murdered honour, loss in wounded courage, weakness creating genius and where genius excels, respectful eyes are raised.

Betrayed, gawped at and worthless, a threat, curse, and joke, outcast majesty submits to death feared yet accepted.
Blindfolded, it's *"Guess who?"* in bloody pranks of Blind Man's Buff, but accepting hatred dissolves its power, excusing more profound than forgiving and obedience meaningless unless love is dismissed as well as embraced.
Dumbfounded by wondrous muddles, his head a ghetto of despair, harshness grating against moonlight, he stammers toward execution spitting blood red and noisy.

STANDING AT SLAMMED DOORS

Teaching failed, message rejected, like trees shattered in hurricanes heroic adventures break the strongest.
In gorgeous gloom the tree casts its leaves, never preserving power, it runs out.
In demented misery, clawing horror and horrible amazement, he shambles toward crucifixion, symbol of scandal generously reserved for traitors, terrorists and *"things that are not."*
More impressive the greatness, less it's appreciated.
Alone and forlorn in the background, with quips and jibes, makeshift humans push in front of him:
   "Come down from your cross!"
   "Stand up for what you believe!"
But anyone who hasn't slipped on dog crap shouldn't scoff at those who have.
From the might of enemies, the weak strike recognition and victims wield influence.
Bearing burdens of insults, garlanded with disgrace, titled blasphemer, drunk, bastard and devil, he's derision in darkness.
Cruelty turning to comedy, *Victim of Galilee* offers himself to be laughed at, but the joke's gone too far.
Nerves quivering in twilight, body broken by doctrinal disagreement, *"No beauty or majesty to attract us to him, nothing in his appearance that we should desire him,"* swallowing insults *"he becomes a worm,"* grizzled Blake, *"to nourish the weak."*
Closing like a flower at approaching dusk – no bees buzzing or small sparrows singing, urine and excrement dribble down twisted legs, flies flitter up and down hollow cheeks, agony haunts downcast eyes.
Bruised, messy, naked and unashamed, he's grizzled victim to pains that can't be soothed, itches that can't be scratched, helpless hands held out – a shrinking creature hiding from our gaze all he will become.

"God is Love" bellow eager Christians.

No! *"God is weakness! God is Pain!"*
Impaled by hatred, he must be scoffed at, abused, laughed at as well as honoured.
Beneath weight of darkness and dust of death, sighing depths of Bach evoke silence
    hushed and breathless.
Weak, he resists pleading for *God's* strength.
Water in sunshine he evaporates, life dipping into filthiness beyond medical sense.
Drowned in doubt, racked with pain, a despairing soul shrieks into the darkness.
No raging defiance, last-minute revelations, glowing faith or comforting texts, but
    irrelevance and meaningless, insignificance and nothingness – the dazzle of
    the grand in the less.
Trembling on a scaffold, *God's* humanness in jagged flesh and gestures of defeat,
    cracked lips sucking cheap wine.

THE DARKENING LAMENT

Hopes dashed, the cry of the child reaches for the woman he has lost.
*"God where are you? Why have you forgotten me? Mummy! Mummy! I can't find you.
    I'm alone. It's dark, please hold my hand:"*
In absence and never-ness, a weakness in need of soft embracing arms.
If only a lamp could be lit, a bed-time story told, a good-night kiss and "don't be afraid,"
    "innocence always calling mutely for protection." 3.
Too late! He's lost himself in people he loved.
Beauty staring everyone in the face is difficult to see.
Mummy gone, protection vanished in devotion exalting powers of weakness, only one
    knowing T*he Adorable* and losing him, finds him again.
Doomed but not deranged, forgotten voices and hidden comforts are yearned for.
Nothing to be snatched, he bleeds like ink onto blotting paper, every globule reeking
    death and distinction.
Sounds of silent farewells hang heavy in the air.
Shrunken, dismembered, a throw-away stub departs with terrible cries, choked sobs,
    hideous sorrow and huddle of haggard women.
No moonlight or starlight but hushed darkness.
Slipping into the unimagined, plodding grandeur forgotten by deity, he discards the
    threadbare cloak of poverty – an ornamental disaster trivialised in loin cloth
    and thorny bonnet hiding quickly silvering hair.
How sad. What if things could be otherwise?

Shapelessly stretched, a body presses against a prickly world.
Victim of failed greatness held high for all to see – a child's sandcastle obliterated at
    high tide, a bubble carried away on the surface of a river, a drooping plant
    begging for water.
The attraction of the rejected – a superfluous "un-person," a faded signpost, torn poster
    stuck to a wall, *"a thing cast away for debris."* 4.
The marvel of it all!
Blacker than black, the grief and monstrous humour of it all – esteemed, mocked and
    never understood, our world never liking its heroes too heroic.

Loss surpassing gain, whatever life makes impressive, must first be made trivial, *"A mighty flame following a tiny spark."* 5.
Hurled into impotence, the weak become powerful – insignificant seeds splintering boulders, microscopic bacteria killing gorillas, reddest poppies sprouting out of cracked concrete and falling leaves leaving new ones in the making, nothing equalling failure for producing aspirations of deepest value.
Strongest helplessness replacing awkward strength, he's Joker in the card-pack, the tip of an iceberg, a small stone altering the face of a large lake – weakness disclosing dignity, superiority maintained in merciful absurdity.
Swaying others by diminishing himself, arriving first by coming last, from timbered cross the container of mystery agitates the world,
an honourable doormat embraces the heart of history,
a *"sombre note that gives the chord its power,"* 6.
"a beautiful object in ruins more beautiful than a beautiful object." 7.
To stay alive, he must be taken away – better losing than winning badly.
Prostrated by necessity, he can't remain.
He must die to discover what death is.
Not a drop disappearing in the sea but the sea absorbed into the drop, a sea so wide that he's straddled centuries.

1. Philip Larkin.
2. "The Battle of Maldon." (Anglo Saxon Poem)
3. Graham Greene.
4. Baudelair
5. Dante.
6. Conrad Aiken.
7. Rodin.

PLAYFULNESS

Bunyan, when the shadow of death had fallen on him, was advised by the Parson of his parish to "drink beer and dance with the girls." Such are the counsels and consolations of the wise.
Dorothy White. The Groombridge Diaries

*He is the embodiment of all that is implied in the word **lila** (play): light, almost ariel activity, boisterous revelry, frivolity, spontaneity, and freedom … Here God plays, posing himself in ecstatic, spontaneous revelry. Here life does not grind along but scampers in dance and rejoices in song. All that makes life in the pragmatic world endurable is to be found here... Here the bondage of necessity does not exist.*
David R. Kinsy

To play is to yield oneself to a kind of magic, to enact to oneself the absolutely other, to pre-empt the future … In play earthly realities become, of a sudden, things of the transient moment, presently left behind, then disposed of and buried in the past; the mind is prepared to accept the unimagined and incredible, to enter a world where different laws apply.
Hugo Rahner. Man at Play

One day while saying his prayers, a Sufi mystic was addressed by God. "Do you want me to tell people what I know about your sins?" The Sufi replied by asking whether he should reveal the extent of His mercy, which if believers knew would make them ignore the Law. "Keep your secret," replied God, "and I'll keep mine."
Sameer Rahim

*I straight returned, and knowing his great birth,
Sought him accordingly in great resorts;
In cities, theatres, gardens, parks and courts:
At length I heard a ragged noise and mirth
Of thieves and murderers; there I him espied …*
George Herbert

PLAYFULNESS

Sharper the focus, greater dismissal of a lugubrious figure plodding Galilean shores, or sombre detainee behind Bible covers.
With no recorded images, a face seen but where?
They *"had no idea who it was,"* shapeshifting in one mode, he vanishes in another, a gardener in Gethsemane, hiker on a rutted road and onlooker at the seashore.
Confounding religious categories now as well as then, he puzzles people.
"Who do people say that I am?" he grizzles in gentle self-mockery.
Escaping pedestals, he saunters streets, exiled, homeless – a three-dimensional figure, complicated and unpredictable, altering forms for different minds.
Speaking spiritual dangers, his thinking contrary to contemporary structures and lifestyle designed to however we imagine it, obtainable but unreachable, I know him, yet I don't!
Obsessed by 'Once upon a time,' *"he escapes me like a truant."* 1.

AN AWAKENING GLIMPSE

Master of the anarchic, quick-witted and provocative voicing impossibilities to provoke thinking,
Solemn joy and gossipy good humour crouch beneath cultural rigidity, his seriousness passing interludes, his humour noisily mistaken for anger.
Young and enthusiastic, *"all things to all men,"* like true spiritual people, he remains a child.
Mystery conjuring familiarity, he behaved then as I hope he would behave now, 'borrowing' figs from neighbourhood trees, leap-frog games by Galilee, skimming stones off flattened water, dawdling in markets fizzing with children and akin to St. Francis, performing metaphorical tricks to distance himself from fashionable religion.
Treating him irreverently frees him from orthodoxy.
Disturbing balances of sobriety, hiding mirth from clerics who cannot cope, he steps aside from religious reality to playful smiles, silently inviting everyone to grin along with him.
Placing no laws on himself, none are thrust on others, a novel figure committed to shock and outrage, freedom of thought, animated ideas and rough and tumble imminence in societies forbidding it – the roguish always brightest and creative.
Controlled yet playful, the lion cub trains for survival,
Freedom the product of disciplined labour not careless irresponsibility, making him strategist of ordered impertinence ridiculing horrors impinging human consciences.
Knavishly irreverent and able to surprise, he disrupts illusions and gate-crashes beliefs, listeners teetering shocked by his doctrinal carelessness.
Independence laced with sly wisdom, rarely answering questions, no gabbled prayers or

rubber-stamped laws shrieking obedience, but more like Plato, playfully indirect in laid-back conversation – a welcomed guest at feasts and festivals where, *"People heard him **gladly**."*
Bypassing religious machinery, he's emotive from dawn's light to day's end, obscurity wedding clarity, play hinged to splendid anger.
Corrupting with kindness, eavesdropping on vices and creating friendships, he exposes God in nodding lilies and miracles of humanness, truth alive in smallest things people do.

LOVEABLE CROOKS

A sneaky question requiring no obligatory answer!
Why do stained-glass saints have soppy faces and unlike literary figures loom colourless and drab?
In contrast, attracting the flawed more than the ritualist, thirty-year old man of street credibility dallies among decadence and depravity, repulsion and repugnance, his friendship with rogues surpassing his patience with aged teachers of religion.
Never apologising for his presence, religious intentions gone astray and bending rules as quickly as possible, a gangster-type hero of playful roughness, impressed by faith in non-believers, dismissing contradictions imposed on simple trust and never urgent to preach, convert and make people holy.
Rejecting superior values, courtesy confronts rogues untrained in religious spitefulness: a comfortable person of reckless friendship whose senseless kindness ransacks alleys crammed with lusty girls of amiable contempt, shifty thieves and religious assassins, mobsters, hellraisers, misfits and good-for-nothing outcasts shy of their God.
Attracted to the underdog, the mucky, rejected people of his world, all of them appeal to the rebel inside him, the most depraved playing peek-a-boo with their chortling babies, the worst pursuing badness believing that it's good.
Comfortable with the non-religious, he never bullies them out of being squalid and profane but making them longing to be clean.
Uncluttered by images of moral superiority, gifted with insight, he sees immortality in ordinary people, feeling things with their senses as much as his own; sinners more easily befriended than the righteously austere.
Beneath distorted faces and moody eyes, goodwill sleeps, inner ruin feeding all that's best, their depravity distorted reflections of love and goodness, most criminals not born but made and everyone better than the crimes they commit.
"They are not good," speculated Dostoyevsky, *"because they don't know they are good...They have to find out, for then they will all at once become good, every one of them."*
Daring words becoming a refreshing change from beliefs in inherent badness.
Every decent story needs a rogue with inability to see things as they are, rogues in a gardening sense, rogue flowers out of place among colour and variety, each one an 'accident' snatched by events beyond their control.

Metal wooed to magnet, he's offers and proposals, his annihilating mercy swamping debts and duties.
Always people not doctrine, individuals never converts, drowning people needing ropes not scolding.
Saints and hoodlums imagined in *Almighty Mind,* waggishly welcomed, tying them to religious rules, little short of treachery.
Less pressure to believe but *Deity* loving everyone as they are, vice being the shortest road to enlightenment.
No finger-wagging indoctrination to decency or bullying into values they aren't aware of.
Never forcing people to embrace his values, his exhilarations, his disgusts – every human being meriting individual recognition, their accidental crimes less annoyance to God than to themselves.
Aware of violations, why yell, *"Sinner!"* evil having to be practised before it can be rejected and wrongdoing making possible finest qualities.
Seeing cheerful violence he bites his tongue, vices of the poor never mentioned, only those of the religious.
Why blame rogues and rebels?
While *"Needs be that offences come,"* most culprits groan, *"I'd avoid them if I could."*
The violent search in the only way they know, worthy people committing crimes only to regret them, nobody wanting to return until they've first gone away and each one sighing secret prayers.
Attempt to make them virtuous and they run for their lives!
Better calls to friendship than dirty fingernails pointing to judgement.

THE UNIMAGINED BECOMING INTIMATE

Ignoring sins, deflecting judgment, in brilliant deceit, he speaks treacherous messages of tolerance, worldly mercy buttonholing ugliness in *"many bad characters,"* not everyone befriending but superstitiously acknowledging.
Relaxed among undesirables, ill at ease among quackery of religion and on nodding terms with murderers and villains, he's man without masks, welcomed not warned off, every squandered past qualifying for favouritisms of pity and clemency.
Never taking sides or efforts to "fit in," but eagerness to belong in absent divisions between 'them' and 'us,' 'we' and 'they,' or 'good' and 'bad.'
No tribal exclusiveness of *"I'm a believer, you aren't,"* as if we need defining by the company we keep; always distinctions without differences, calling both friends and enemies by their first names.

Disparities ignored, with gasps of admiration, he idles among heathen goodness in playful disrepute.
Avoiding pious sterility, a man of litter-blown suburbs, markets, ghettos and mean streets crammed with criminality, none as sordid as we imagine, everyone trying to climb upwards, small holes making fine lace attractive, wet pavements reflecting lights of faraway stars.

Behind every felon a victim, none beyond repair, no one hating God but searching the little they know and believing all they can, not what they should.
Capacities for wickedness wield capacities for good, ideas of evil probably less than evil.
Forgiveness offered, never demanded, all lives instinctively spiritual, none straying beyond clumsy mercy, his friendship ignoring innumerable crimes, his generosity over-tipping all who don't deserve it.
"I was once a blasphemer, persecutor and violent man," grizzled one ex-criminal, "but I was shown mercy because I acted in **ignorance and unbelief**."
Divinity dozing in bottomless depths, kindness saturating badness, everyone possessing secret wishes to reach beyond themselves.
As grubs become insects, all programmed for change.
A hidden yearning and *"good for nothing"* 2. lower kind of happiness in buried ideals impossible to see and understand.
An imprint, signature and *Inner Light* alive in all, especially the unaware.
No divine mark would mean no existence, but God burnt into every soul, pricking out warts and windflowers, blackheads and apple blossom, sunshine sneaking through smallest windows flooding darkest rooms.

INTO ATTRACTIVE DANGER

*"I will put my law in their **inward** parts,"*
"A piece of divinity in man," insisted Thomas Browne, everyone hearing calls and receiving invitations, then, when the pupil is ready, teacher appears.
Expansively Present One awakening the sleeping, none deserving the worst.
Between crime and restraint, souls jolted into beguiling affections, a love for children, father, mother, wife, dog – smidgens of love pervading everyone, the worst touched with pity aiding friends in illness – Atheists, Muslims, Hindus, terrorists and everyone else tearfully devoted to their children.
*"If you being evil do kind things and give presents to your children, **how much more will God** ..."*
Loving by being loved, playful mercy infuses obscenity and sanctity, smallest sparks arousing light, multitudes following without realising, rain weeping equally on toadstools and bluebells.
Snooping into minds, rogues are cheered to make them better.
No heroes or villains but souls befriended in twilight gravity, none frightened into the fold, berated to change or barricaded out of this life and the next, for what breed of *Deity* births souls to forever inflict them?

Flirting with the underworld, only a conspirator, *"one of the roughs,"* 3. found among the worst and accused of *"friendliness with criminals,"* could flounce among gangdom without contacts secret introductions and friendships. 4.
Rejecting religious isolationism, masquerading as crime among criminals, loss of reputation is inevitable.
How does he do it?
Reserved and respectable, I'm answerless.

Maybe he's more tactical, less serious or more humorous than me, for in tension and conflict humour becomes a comforting reminder of shared humanity.
"Happy are you," he rattled, *"when people denounce your name as criminal."*
Praising nuisances, rascality grabs him, fiendishness more interesting than smug morality.
Playful sleuth of backward glance glimpsing light in squalid corners, stands uncondemning among swindlers and everyone like himself living by their wits.
In twinkle-eyed mischief, *"Neither do I condemn you,"* aware as he is that those to whom evil is done, do evil in return.
Sympathy for the nondescript, short comings are ignored, bad behaviour not always their own fault, every villainy prompting yearnings for higher things, none rescued by punishing them.
"Kindness leading to repentance," he calls them out of condemnation imposed upon themselves.
Ransacking tradition, pity surpasses punishment, a singing bird careless of listeners, an absent-minded executioner who'd lie for someone they loved.
"Believing all things, hoping all things," he glimpses goodness time had given and rudely snatched away.

HUMBUG AND HOLINESS

Unlike po-faced followers, no rebukes for naughtiness or blinkered accusations of guilt.
Loitering among evil, he hoodwinks into good, playfully reversing worst and worthless.
Mid disturbance and contradiction, disparities dwindle between obnoxious thief and vindictive believer, detected crimes and secret ones.
Oh dear! How we hurl our stones with brimming enthusiasm, obsessive righteousness more threatening than inspiration.
Better dashes of decadence than humble pomposity, intelligent pretence and farcical sainthood, lines alarmingly narrow between slouchy crook and purveyor of 'white lies,' smug righteousness and furious wickedness, excessive rules producing lawlessness, adamant beliefs spawning intolerance.
In glorified treason, atheists as close to God as cocksure believers, lawbreakers paying penance for born-again bumptiousness, rogues scapegoats for fictitious holiness, criminals exposing sins believers concealing them – the 'elect' not so exclusive as they think,
Prompting naughty thoughts of *"many that are first shall be last; and the last, first,"* admirably illustrated by a party thrown for a scoundrel who ran away instead of glowing examples of one who stayed at home.
Everyone a rascal in one way or another, saints failing to be recognised if there were no sinners, no wise thinkers if there were no fools and if it wasn't for maligned Judas, none would get a look-in.
How easy labelling people evil than having one's principles shaken, every 'outsider' a necessity providing 'insiders' luxuries of faith.
Ruined by criminality, failing to come to terms with their crimes, faithless offenders become saviours in saving ignorance:

Expiating offerings for professional self-sacrifice of the devout, atonements for double standards of righteous respectability, deficits for peacockery of imagined humility, such attitudes putting *Deity* in a bad mood and prompting angels to poke out pink tongues.

EXTRAVAGANT VIRTUE

Happy believers synonymous with rampant criminals?
This is playfulness bordering on roguery!
He must be joking but he isn't, true and false playfully overlapping one another, everyone victims of God's forgetfulness.
Maybe he needs rescuing from friends as well as enemies?
Every believer hiding enormities of misleading honesty and empty purity,
> bartering one kind of righteousness for another,
> demanding good behaviour impossible to give,
> picking out facts to suit their own thesis and
> when it comes to money, the holiest turning a blind eye!

Behaviour appearing right is often wrong, every smug feeling a trap, over-zealous dedication inflicting irreparable damage, history's wisest king sighing, *"There's **not** a righteous person on earth who does what is right and never sins."*
Among the worst, he magnifies masquerades of the devout, wrongdoing less destructive than pretension.
Sometimes better trusting the unworthy than the over-zealous insistence of the well-meaning, enemies often more honest than friends, rogues exuding virtues, worldly-wise putting religion to shame, dark dwellers possessing more common sense than light bringers and mock modesty of sainthood driving the rest of us to borders of crime!
Playing with criminality, *"the fall furthers the flight."* 5.
Weary of regulations, he playfully shouts, *"I tell you, use worldly wealth to gain friends for yourselves."*
Or, be artful yet reasonable, eager but reflective.
Say that again!
He does, implying that it's neater being an inventive rogue than a religious bore:
> *"And his master **admired the rascality of the servant because he had reacted reflectively**, for the sons of this world are for their own generation **more reflective than the sons of light.**"*

Less indigestible dogma more *real people* – honey squeezed from all kinds of flowers.
Everyone requesting a candle, offered a chandelier.
Romans, Samaritans, Gentiles and the world's debris invited to belong.
A woman eroding a judge's legal authority.
Villainous servants threatened with dismissal.
Lazy men given full pay.
Calculating scoundrels receiving warmest handshakes.
Imposters sowing weeds in a neighbour's garden.
Heaping rewards on someone possessing stolen goods.
Naughty ladies promised brightest destinies.

Striking friendships with occupying enemies rather than fellow countrymen.
Vagrants, prostitutes and psychopaths, conniving their way to holier things.
Theatricals end, curtains close, smiling, hand in hand, ugly sisters join Cinderella on stage to prolonged acclaim.
Villains heartily applauded as well as innocent hero prompting shock surprise loitering in the wing.
After all, scoundrels acted their treachery stupendously.
Does it matter whose worst or best as long as all are in?
It's part of life's play!
If appointed a respectable Cinderella, be thankful – it could easily be the other way around!

PLEASURES OF THE OBVIOUS

Now he's *"wining and dining!"*
Party invitations from the prestigious, my question being, *"Why not me?"*
His party-going discredited him as Christian, in past legalistic days my *"No"* qualified me!
But why be 'good' when missed things never happen again?
Smug innocence diminishes humour, while in his company people became all that nobody expected them to be,
"Simple cheery sinners" 6. awarded freedom to trust their intuition, dismiss religion or nurture it, live sensibly or hurtle off the rails – *Deity* relishing our attention while respecting our refusals.
Chess pieces litter the table, it's up to everyone how they are positioned, no one acquiring authority to impose rules on others, none advancing by disciplined disapproval, everyone free who give their liberty to others.
In jingly pleasure, Philosopher steps from desk to nursery floor to play with kittens.
Every person dragged from reverence to dalliance, virtuous frivolity to capering kindness.
Give him Lego bricks and second-hand toys, bragging atheists and howling preachers and he plays!

What things amused him and was he told off for laughing?
Denying both is evidence by absurd assumptions.
"And when Jesus heard he laughed," records gnostic Gospel of Judas – he couldn't make fun of people without making fun of himself.
There are different ways of laughing, not all facial.
If he didn't laugh easily, he never laughed at all, if he had no sense of humour, a bad joke has been played on us.
People are judged by their laughter or lack of it.
Did he laugh at himself – laughter a saving grace and letting-go.
We expect him to be sober and sedate – he ought to be but he isn't, like artist Frans Hals, he's *"Master of the laugh."*

Seriousness clinging to wit, smiling never sneering, laughter irrepressible and liberating, his grins as well as his words suggest seditious possibilities infringing narrow-mindedness.
Provoking laughter provokes thought, absence of humour is lostness, both being underestimated gifts creating historic leaps and bounds.
No mention of either, but neither hints of him relieving himself behind a rock.
Lowering stress levels, his laughter so frequent, his jokes inspirational, why bother!

Lofty truths hobnob simple pleasures in wedding feasts and verbal games.
In disorderly song and music, hilarity without consequences, celebrations without goals, wine spiked with twirling dance and disregard of dignity as books of law are swapped for idiotic looks of good nature.
He undoubtedly danced, enjoyed music, played games and exchanged jokes – humans need these luxuries.
Simple enjoyments, innocent play and bubbled laughter, purest evidence of truth and antidotes to pride making old things young again.
Now it's cutlery and conversation, garrulous yells and chirping gaiety.
Merry mead gurgles in his throat.
A twinkling 'wickedness' and devil-may-care absurdity, everyone dithering in un-programmed happiness.
"Stop it Jesus. Remember your decorum. Enthusiasm makes enemies!"
But humorous and comfortable, he refuses to take religion as seriously as we do.

A LICENSE TO BE SILLY

Unlike pioneers of causes refusing to be humorous, he's swept away by important trivialities.
Because of his seriousness he's not being serious.
Emptied of formulas, irresponsible as bird song, a panoply of fun among ragged children, fingers up noses, thumbs in mouths.
"Cast away childish things," demanded St. Paul.
"Become a child," he contradicts in unbecoming insolence.
The first leading to boredom, the second to teddy bears, football, ice cream and numerous neurotic amusements lost as we get older, holier and wiser.
"Don't grow up – it's a trap," announced a shop sign, everyone needing playful silliness, less authority and no moralising judgment.
This man excels in jokey aphorisms, mischievous criticism and flinty jests of despair at anyone violating simplicities.
In possession of himself he surrenders to everything and anaesthetising the ordinary, light is hurled into concealed places.
"A guide, restful and leisurely," observed Gnostic writer of the Gospel of Truth.
Travelling casually, energies attract not compel.
Playfully irritating, *"My way of life is easy,"* he quips, *"my burdens light-hearted."*
Or *"More difficult than self-denial. is reckless enjoyment."*
   "Following me you might break down with grief, but you'll leap up singing!"

But why isn't he seen apart from his cross and how would he have acted living to old age, parchment skin and ash grey hair?

HE'S NOT A HUMAN SUNDAY

His message is pleasure as well as pain, every stab playfully piercing irrationality and irreverent outrageousness.
Why is he expected to condemn people and who conceived austerity as the stamp of spirituality?
Why are holy loonies bent on bashing baddies and pious believers preferring judge, jury and executioner?
A religion of penalties, indulged corruption deserving fiercest judgment, despotic deity getting even, settling scores and threatening punishment.
Aren't they aware that no one beckoned by mercy can be shattered by judgement?
Impishly declaring that no one is rejected who is already embraced, he metaphorically trills: *"Are you coming out to play? Come on, walk with me!"*
Who wants rabid warnings and tactless threats of hell?
Better someone cooing, *"All shall be well."*
Nerve is needed – this happiness is scary and heretical, but better irrational spontaneity than exaggerated sobriety and sanctified indictments.
Never ascending to the pulpit, he's glad, and glad people can't abuse and exact misery.
In appetites for experience, he grabs his cake and eats it.
"Go on, laugh," he twitters, *"When I'm forgotten, you might remember."*
Running rings around the clueless, witty planner of realities uproots heavy dogma to play consequences – sacred uniting with secular in pain and pleasure.

WINE OF WEDDING WISDOM

Wedding guest, weary of sensibility, performs a naughty miracle weighted with risk, a case of no wonders without natural phenomenon.
Dismissing austerities, he plans to make things human, his pragmatism simplifying possible complications.
Miracles of common sense can be amusing, seeing problems and comprehending remedies before embarrassment arises.
Imagination akin to miraculous playtime, with conjurer's flourish and magician's jugglery, holy novelty slips down his sleeve in celebratory indulgence.
In lightest things debonair charm and spiritual authority is seen.
Staring at water in transcendent idiocy, grins float to the surface, smiles steal across his face.
An appropriate wink, a dabbled finger, he stirs, sucks, smiling so wide rotting teeth are glimpsed.
Restraint can be stressful.
Like circus acts, if everyone's not careful, doves might fly from top hats!
Brimming beakers filled from vats of affection, in carefree behaviour and sumptuous plates of wit and humour, awe and glee yell at each other as the room becomes bigger.

Delivered from busyness, I hear gush of conversation, chug of laughter, screech of
fiddle and eruptions of irrelevance as flushed revellers spill wines of pleasure
and wisdom around tables and chairs.
Happiness has become unbearable and he's eager to share it, *"Three things being gifts
of the Almighty,"* quipped Irish poet, Raferty, *"poetry, dancing and principle."*
On the heels of revellers comes the minstrel, frowns turning to irrepressible merriment,
witty conversation louder, drinking songs jollier, dancing livelier and seizures
giddier intoxicating body and soul – it's difficult keeping pace with such
enthusiasm.
In solemn silliness with tensions of mystery and comic unpredictability, water changes to
wine as cows change grass to milk and pumpkins transfigure to coach and
horses.
"Do it again Jesus! Do it again!"
With outsiders eager to gate-crash, breathless, we must depart, Dante's final vision
being sight of one who *loves and smiles.*
Disorder and gaiety has defied absurdity, absence of experts making everything obvious
– always alternative ways of receiving truth than loud persuasion.
Life's important decisions could be trivial ones, every failure stimulating knowledge of
who we are.
Flippancy less harmful than seriousness, a sense of the ridiculous a saving grace
spilling sumptuous importance into the nonsense of our days.
Beyond threats, sanctions and unwritten warnings, enjoyments become virtues too
heavy to tamper with, happiness, emotions we needn't recover from and things
playfully done worth doing again and again.
Making light of sobriety, *Party Person* won't be robbed of pantomime flummery,
grimacing jest and throw-away wonders, making him *Enjoyer* as well as *Seer*,
more down-to-earth than his followers, especially earnest ones.
Illicit as winds and tides, nicest kind of doctor, friendliest breed of dog, he's soul of the
party, more hidden from Christian views supporting him than godless views
opposing him.

FLIRTING WITH WORDS

Multiple stories wrapped in question marks, meanings sometimes withheld, he's into
word games!
With pauses and hesitations, *"they marvelled at his **words of charm**."*
Lips sealed with secrets, his thinking not always understood must be 'reached after.'
Never patronising or straight forward, puckish, whimsical and lover of allegory better
suited for humorous people, he **plays** with friends and enemies, scattering
stories of life and *Good Old God*.
No preachiness, more tricky word pictures and caricature proclaiming obscure ideas
telling people to embrace all they don't know and press on from there.
Flummoxing audiences with taunting paradox, humorous stories and the oil of repartee,
he shouts at the hard of hearing, voicing one thing, cunningly meaning another,
half revealing, half concealing, truth vibrant in one place hidden in another, all

we aren't intended to understand and all we need to revealing verbal strategy and spiritual insight.
*"He said **nothing** without parables."* Begging a clear moral message, they wouldn't get it.
Beyond logic, syllables alive with suggestions and sensations promising more than they reveal, *Magician of Allegory*, reveals himself in chosen words, his scattered clues abstract pictures, his hurl-away remarks void of dogmatic precision.
Less sermons more one-liners in playful implications, listeners are abandoned to uncertainty and suspense, his riveting sentences less explanation, more suggestion.
Shaping stories from people's lives in their levels of development, he abandons listeners to view themselves in degrees of light that they see.
Never pontificating, eloquently unconventional, riddle-ish in anecdote, rousing in rhetoric, he escapes religious certainties, his verbal trickery easy to remember yet hard to understand.
Oozing sorrowful fun, impossible truths none cast in steel, are all frittered away to listener level.
If true, his playfulness is terrifying!

STUBBON ABSENCE OF CONFORMITY

Manipulating rules, he abandons them, rules restricting him as they restrict themselves.
Truant dodging school, with pointed repartee the solemn are ridiculed, like Socrates, playing games with his accusers, the smugly virtuous and blandly vain.
Poking fun he debunks martyred smiles and arrogant correctness sneaking in back door blabbing unhelpful advice.
Never appearing sillier than when they're serious, he lampoons high-placed leaders policing morals and ducking under grave pretence, glimpsing in their eyes the misery of their ideas.
Struck by silliness, two fingers rise at bustling pomposity, pointless gobbledegook and reckless hypocrisy.
Raising eyebrows, eyes alight with audacity and taunting in fervour, he inappropriately teases: *"Prostitutes will enter the kingdom in front of you!"*
Jest in earnest, red-light ladies snatching leads from the professionally religious!
See him! Hear him!
Galilee man won't be held back!
Shock tactics of astonishing value suggest why talk when you can laugh?

BUSTLING CONCEIT AND YAH BOO MOCKERY

Playfully disgruntled with a finely tuned sense of the ridiculous, he mocks men in pompous clothes, all dressed but nowhere to go.
Wackily joking, *"Waiter! There's a fly in my camel soup. Strain it!"* Soup is swallowed, camel humps, knobbly knees, cleft feet and all!
Toying with words, humour re-thinking law, he cartoons fumblers picking specks from people's eyes when logs dangle from their own.

Truth, appealing by distortion, wisdom conjoining amusement, he bellows the absurd:
> "It's easier for a camel to go through a needle's eye than a rich man to enter the kingdom;" oriental comicality of "the cow jumped over the moon and the dish ran away with the spoon," playful attitudes to earnest beliefs the only way of making sense of them.

Defrosting arrogance, humour demolishes without malice raising few smiles from people bolted together rather than born, knowing everything but feeling nothing.

Treading toward banana skin moments, each one invented then, would be ignored now.

Whimsy and melodrama flicker inside him.

Dashing into crowds twirling skirts of gusto and rage, institutions rocked.

Religion tottered clumsy and confused, intrusive theology clashed with playful tyranny, couldn't care-less forces collided with immoveable masses.

Never wondering, "Is this wise?" he crows, *"What description can I find for such people? Bloody-minded louts, you're impossible to please. We played dance music but you stayed in your seats. We sang requiems but you wouldn't mourn. Pride always justifies its inconsistencies."*

In singing he surely *felt*.

A soloist inviting duets but no one's interested.

Flutist announces dance, no one moves a metre leaving him to shimmy alone in austerity and pleasure.

> *"Jesus the dancer's master is,*
> *A great skill at the dance is his,*
> *He turns to right, he turns to left,*
> *All must follow his teaching deft."* 7.

Does no one realise that foolish feelings are pinnacles of spirituality?

None called to success, everyone designed to be slightly stupid.

SHRUG OF SHOULDERS, PINCH OF SALT

Begging cures for her sick daughter, a foreigner receives churlish replies: *"I was sent to help Jews not Gentiles. Why snatch crusts from babies and toss them to dogs?"*

Criticising because he admires, *playful* duels commence.

Gruffness disguising vulnerability, no grizzled tongue but coy winks, artful repartee and double meanings yelped in jest that dare not be said seriously, scholar playfully teasing pupil in cat and mouse banter until the joke is grasped.

Goose-girlish and gushing, she grabs with pinch of salt what's recognised in drollery – like humouring the elderly by letting them get the better of you.

This man is groomed for playdom and given to nicknames.

Intimacy justifies nicknames, all of us called by who we are, nicknames wielding wisdom as well as humiliation.

Flattering power with fibs, Peter is nicknamed Rocky; comic prophecy gummed to one who wasn't but would become, like calling a stout man Slim, a tall man Shorty – one stab of humour worth sessions of counselling.

Verbally rough, teasing becomes tests.

Pernickety brothers James and John are Sons of Thunder – rumbling grumps until irritable spells are broken.
In good-tempered tyranny, inglorious wrongs become mock-worthy signs of the potentially correct.
Jumping before pushed, the elephant threatened by the mouse, he plays with the powerful who shrink from appearing fools.
Devilment and roguery stand out in animal insults, spoilt child Herod becoming, *"That fox!"*
Unreasoning and insolent, a boo-hiss tyrant never to be given charge of infant schools.
Comic grotesquery of one who, *"Stole to his throne like a fox, ruled like a tiger, and died like a dog,"* scoffed 1st century Josephus.
Only shrewd humour records historical condemnation and better a nickname than a number
Healthy souls make fun of seriousness, a "go-ahead" to destroy monsters, "tickling them to death" until "sides split with laughter."
If life is part of play, *Grand Himself* plays in pleasure and pain.
Parents play with babies, poets with words, pianists with keys, scientists with concepts.
Hearts are put into play – *Everlasting One* collects hearts!

STOMPING HOME FORGIVEN

Textual symbols of bliss in dawn after darkness is the spreading heedlessness of *"boys and girls **playing** in the streets."*
Girlhood and boyhood dancing with Deity.
Shapeless Profundity shouting happy endings, when scripts of life play out in silly happiness and fiercest beliefs etched in stone become hilariously obsolete, our smiling friend rewarding runaways for the pain of their falling instead of condemning them for having fallen.

1. *Flemish Benguine.*
2. *Iris Murdoch.*
3. *Kenneth Grahame.*
4. *An idea from Joel Oliver.*
5. *George Herbert.*
6. *Walt Whitman.*
7. *Gerardus van der Leeuw.*

FEMININITY

Jesus was a great aristocrat … It takes a great aristocrat to be capable of great tenderness and gentleness and unselfishness; the tenderness and gentleness of strength.
D. H. Lawrence

Thus Jesus Christ, who does good against evil is our very mother. We have our being in him where the ground of Motherhood begins; with all the sweet keeping of love that endlessly follows … For where the soul is highest, noblest and most worshipful, there it is lowest, meekest and mildest.
Julian of Norwich

The little urchin with the gold-red hair, whom I have just watched toddling past my house; her hair shall not be cut short like a convict's; no, all the kingdoms of the earth shall be hacked about and mutilated to suit her. She is the human and sacred image; all around her the social fabric shall sway and split and fall, the pillars of society shall be shaken, and the roofs of ages come rushing down and not one hair on her head shall be harmed.
G. K. Chesterton

You can never imagine what it is to have a man's force of genius in you and yet to suffer the slavery of being a girl.
George Elliot. Daniel Deronda

Then Andrew began to speak, and said to his brothers:
"Tell me, what do you think of these things she has been telling us?
As for me, I do not believe that the teacher would speak like this.
These ideas are too different from those we have known."
And Peter added:
"How is it possible that the teacher talked in this manner with a a woman about secrets of which we ourselves are ignorant?
Must we change our customs and listen to this woman?
Did he really choose her, and prefer her to us?"
The Gnostic Gospel of Mary Magdalene

FEMININITY

How apologetic describing him as he-man,
Toxically masculine with points to prove,
The Clark Kent hero dashing into church and changing into Superman.
What good is strength without wisdom?
Nowadays, the strong need help more than the weak.
Feminine in feeling, masculine in mind – two natures in nearness, impossible to be man
without woman, broad shoulders cannot disguise hidden femininity and
defenceless infancy sucking the nipples of Mary.
Hard-wired for empathy, femininity births masculinity in conundrum and mystery, *touch*
and *feel* linking chivalry to womanhood, macho scepticism to female
sentimentality and maleness to feminine mystery.
Tiptoeing out of the incomprehensible, vulnerable to violence, gentle Seer scatters
Illogical wisdom in his world,
A desecrated victim of bitter-sweet passivity in whose eyes lurk the unconscious and
unknown, feminine *anima* the guide and go-between inner and outer worlds.
Emptied of self-sufficiency, *"skin stretched over tenderness,"* 1. quiet symmetry
surpasses burly spirituality.

UNION OF OPPOSITES

Curiously remote yet appealing,
In jarring contrast to blokeish arrogance, testosterone stamina and butch swagger so
alien to *"little girl hope,"* 2. femininity hesitantly reveals itself in altruism and
sacrifice.
Male action linked to female bravery and nuance, he violates convention chatting openly
with women, confiding in them, freeing their voices, congratulating them in
public, a king them his friends and unlike his followers, never parking them in
sidings for doctrinal reasons, convinced as he is that men are equal to women
more than women to men!
Atrociously transparent, quick in apprehensions, he weeps in public – the grief of
farewell, pathos of a lifted suitcase, final embrace, dribble of falling tears and
departing train hurrying a loved-one away – the feminine ever sensitive to grief
and loss.
But why no woman in da Vinci's "Last Supper?"
Why no supremacy for Magdalene Mary, leading lady at an empty tomb?
In God's eye, everyone's deepest soul being a woman.
If man imagines himself head, woman becomes queen, men bent on
accomplishment, woman eager to understand, extracting male conceit and
surrendering to self-examination.
Fathers speakers, mothers listeners in immutable sincerity and absence of ego, his
mummy heart dashingly alive in drop-out people occupying lonely places.

Perceiver of the forgotten, the misunderstood and violated, he dandles dribbling
>babies, Never denying his vulnerability, pushing for equality, he kisses his
>betrayer. Pitying pregnant women he populates the solitude of the sick –
>mercy and forgiveness repudiated practises in his day, feminine freedom to
>think highlighting our own.

THE ASTONISHMENT OF LOVE

Poetic and pathetic, giving without grabbing, he's *"moved with compassion."*
Shamelessly tough, men not expected to express deep feelings but seeking like man
>he receives like woman touching lives with girlish hands, hidden purity drawn
>out by motherly understanding.
Imitating maternal in protective reserve, discreet with his own pain, he copies God
>our mother despairing over all we do to one another, his every affection
>characterised by woman in finest instincts of psychic sympathy soothing,
>restorative and sensitive to emotional values; distinct humility, listening
>sadness and transformative anger uniquely expressing his feelings.
Held back and passed over, in lady-like devotedness that won't be grabbed, he suffers
>female alienations of male prejudices – the woman betrayed, willing to endure
>and seeing hope when her lover wearies of her.
A dogged loyalty that attentively waits, grieving over unreasonable ambitions, excusing
>errors in words, looks, gestures and pleading abandonment of journeys toward
>self-destruction.

WOMAN – MIRROR OF MAN

In love that renounces and woman abused, masculine knows itself in feminine, his
>femininity a mirror, seeing himself in respectful pity, subtleness, fragility and
>necessary defiance.
Never discriminating or reducing women to minor roles, he's eternal feminine and
>confident possessor of compulsive powers when choosing to wield them.
Self-effacement possessing him in Mona Liza's silence and hesitant smile, in
>evasiveness, absence of grasp, impenetrable mystery plus something more.
As much *her* than *him,* restless music contrasts law chiselled in stone.
Hating intrigues, detesting manoeuvring, and wielding no power over others, tender
>intentions are always encouraged; like marriage, wooing before winning,
>cultivating instead of coercing, inviting never conscripting.
Dismissing elaborate artificiality, he's motherlove making wise choices, showing
>patience with the weak lest he shatter their image.
Intuitive and emotional – avoiding disturbing the helpless who partly know, he overlooks
>faults, deriving no satisfaction in anyone's humiliation and never triumphing in
>another's loss.
No iced water hurled over others' successes, spoiling their sense of fun or discouraging
>pleasure he never had, but hooked to loss instead of certainty, always *"Oops"*
>at adorable errors and majestic failures.
Bewildered sometimes by who he really is, vulnerabilities whimper in feminine rejection,
>self-doubt and exhaustion.

MUTUAL INTELLECT AND AFFECTION

Perceiving life's mysteries, imprisoning with intuitive glances, he's a veil revealing as much as it conceals.
Complex yet interesting, a feminine sense of strangeness and infinitude, eager to please yet desperate for affection.
Listening eyes glance as a woman glances – secret watcher more than nosy onlooker, pretending nothing but who he is.
Kind to himself and others in lady-like love for man and balm for masculine despair, he could have written letters from a woman's heart.
Conscious of the burden of gender, he's devotion of the unrequited with a heart for small things men take for granted – no pushy advances but patiently awaiting.
Giving much, expecting nothing, courtesy eclipses anger and sincerity of spirit creates impressive appearances.

WOOING AND WINNING

"You must be born again," bleat heated preachers, he the feminine womb of being and motherly presence of God closest to humanity, courageously sacrificing happiness embracing her child's interests and watching son or daughter depart knowing they'll never return – always looking, always hoping.
"Behold my mother!" himself existing in far-seeing perceptions, discernment and a sixth sense deficient in men.
"Men loving with their eyes, women with their ears," 3. for him, heights, depths of threatening simplicity and extravagance in moderation.
Tender among grinding ferocity, an unresisting body folds in grief, a slip of fragility strengthless to do anything, love becoming defenceless in pleading hands of feminine victims whose rights have been crushed:
A used-up lady, voice silenced, body violated, and carelessly discarded as object and thing.
Desperate for affection he touts for tenderness, needs certainty, craves sympathy and falters famished for acceptance.
His loss is a lap to sit on, a mother's hand clasped tight and cherished whispers swishing like breezes in meadows.
The nursling of Mary, man-child of motherly desire and sisterly feeling, every attribute complimentary to man while representing woman.
Sitting well with feminine equality, I refrain toying with Balzac's quip that, *"Woman's virtue is man's greatest invention,"* but *"disruptively female,"* 4. he's the voice of waterfalls in courage, psychic awareness and uncomplaining demise.
"She-ness" balancing "he-ness," a woman saviour no dogma to shout but mercy to strew – giving all, claiming little, caring while wanting to be cared for.

Muscular do-gooding cannot diminish inner womanhood, every word hallmarked by insight and diffidence – filigree qualities more ravishing than painted domes of temple and palace.

Critics might detect Sissy, teacher's pet, mummy's darling, blubbering over a run-down city, picking flowers and shaking them childishly in the air!
"But sorry, I can't help it. Blessed are the useless!"

Teaching people to fail better, he treads inadequacy, choosing blessing and hallowing to blasting and cursing, sins of the sincere to bowed heads of the devout.
No religion of sainted death-bed departures, but quaintest paradox, imitating mother drenched in long looks, acts of resignation, gifted intuition, kept secrets, gifted listening and suppressed disappointments.
Maybe *"We're all meant to be mothers of God, for God always needs to be born."* 5.

FEEL OF APPLE BLOSSOM HANDS

Female in feeling, he befriends a lady with seeping blood.
No clanging rebuke at Peter's denials but mummy severity running across rooms like sunshine on water.
Hauled from her love nest by voyeur's feigning humility, sexual errors are never spotlighted.
Not looking her up or down, his constraint dazzles!
Competent to hurl a stone, he refuses, blaming the woman doesn't absolve the man.
No lectures, harsh rebukes or moral warnings, penance and good behaviour not required for forgiveness.
His feminine side betrays him; with sisterly nods, gratuitous hands wave in darling mercy: *"Go away and be a good girl,"* a verbal curtesy floating like smiles from passing strangers.
Understanding her passions helps her suffer less from them.
No long speeches but superb unconcern and outrageous leniency, *"What is done is done, now move on."*
Such eloquence, delicacy and outrageous compliance – never meddling with morals or inferring inferiority, he refuses to judge.
This man is a cameo of courtesy, a moral puzzle, his eyes whispering everything's all-right when it isn't.
Erasing blushes as quickly as possible, passive as the bow between a violinist's fingers, a woman's heart speaks.
Perfectly poised, comfortably sombre amongst sex, severity and malicious satisfaction at the damnation of others, vengeance is reeked in feathery forbearance.
Never punishing anyone for bad behaviour, he knows that disobedience creates its own punishment.
Femininity surpassing lawgiving, happy weaknesses are swept away leaving him doodling in dust crudest cartoons of gob-smacked accusers and Judges void of understanding.
Grim solemnity is impressive, male authority formidable, but femininity mimics *Divine Vastness* disguised as mother and child.

LOOKS OF EVERLASTINGNESS

Once a boy, now a father, I pause before womanly mystique with terrible consequences. Preserver of creaturehood among masculine insensitivity, he's winner of emotions before possessor of minds, prolonged compassion etched into defenceless looks, giver of newness to all who gaze inside themselves, *"everyman's soul being a woman before God."* 6.
"Beholding the man," prefigures human experience in Beatrice guide, Sophia wisdom, tender maid and mother, *"Sorrow with her family of sighs,"* 7. and Pain Bearer in whose dying the world was widowed.

1. *Vernon Sproxton.*
2. *Charles Peguy.*
3. *Thomas Hardy.*
4. *Diana Wood Middlebrook.*
5. *Meister Eckhart.*
6. *Coventry Patmore.*
7. *Shelley.*

SENSUALITY

Sensuous: *relating to the senses without implication of lasciviousness or grossness … pleasing to the senses, alive to the pleasures of sensation; connected with sensible objects (of pleasure) experienced through the senses.*
Chambers Dictionary

*What we call wit they (the French) call **esprit**- spirit. When they want to call a man witty, they call him **spirituel**. They actually use the same word for wit which they use for the Holy Ghost.*
G. K. Chesterton

*The devout person does not only believe but **feels** there is a Deity. They have **actual sensations** of Him!*
Addison

*Dearly Beloved! I have called you so often and you have not heard me.
I have shown myself to you so often and you have not seen me.
I have made myself fragrance so often, and you have not smelled me,
savorous food, and you have not tasted me.
Why can you not reach me through the object you touch
or breathe me through sweet perfumes?
Why do you not see me? Why do you not hear me?
Why? Why? Why?*
Ibn 'Arabi (Sufi. 12th century)

I should like to have a great ale-feast for the King of Kings; I should like the Heavenly Host to be drinking it for all eternity.
Irish. Author unknown. 10th century

Man will hereafter be called to account for depriving himself of the good things which the world lawfully allows.
Abba Arika

Live, live, all you can … Live!
Henry James. The Ambassadors

SENSUALITY

Hurling himself into life, enjoyment occurred in unexpected places.
Reverently described as holy but why not *sensual*?
Embracing blood and brain, bone and sinew, primal urge plus something more, He savours beauty without discussing it.

Emotions more suggested than stated, turbulent man performs riotous roles with Philosopher's jest, mystic's imagination and Zen strategy, his social awkwardness making him the anticipation of un-read books, a work of art less understood than sensed.
Never addled by notions of justification, substitution and predestination, earliest marble images overlook bleeding wounds, gaunt crosses and crucifixions.
Seizing every day for its uniqueness, uncluttered realism hangs about him, states of feeling in contrast to Bible intellect – more in common with Plato than structuralism of St. Paul.
Loitering among peasants and the great unwashed, opens a manuscript to be studied, re-read, passed on or thrown away.
Traveller to unknown places, what kind of stories did he tell himself?
If only he'd kept a journal, putting pen to paper would have shaped meanings: describing ordinariness we'd marvel at extraordinariness, but rough hands are not given to written words and aware that deepest spirituality isn't understood by reading about it, writing is resisted.
Overmuch detail spoils fun as well as adding to it, thankfully leaving us to fabricate books of whoever we intend him to be.
But why Biblical silence, gaps and unblushing dumbing down, earliest writers avoiding the lighter sides of his character.
Were there sinister agendas and editorial tweaking, his knowing looks, winks, smiles, shrugs and nods too provocative to describe?
Abounding in leisure as well as busy in ministry, why aren't we told that he **enjoyed himself**?
A myriad sensations now lost or thrown away.
Outrageous heartiness, kind-natured naughtiness diluted to humourless statements and leaden thought beyond the grasp of those who collated the details.
Refusing to formulate texts, followers did the job for him, some utterances mere religious propaganda.
Or maybe silence proves inspiration – a brake on busybody curiosity, leaving him best understood by the silence he keeps.
Knowing too little than too much, imagination is a must!

PERFECT ORDER DISTURBED

Goodness becoming dullness, textbooks dubious, gusto clung to poise, enormity mingled with informality.

Embracing the senses, no smug virtues but un-calculating openness like love that can't
	be taught – *Deity* never realised by suppression of sensuality but by raising it.
Emptied of cant, exchanging 'fixed things' for the improbable plus no repressed
	instincts, *Galilean Youth* dances his own dance and sings his own song,
	sighing as often as he smiles.
Man of luxurious sensations and absence of usualness, his over-stating best winked at
	and always taken for granted.
Sensuality essential to art, he exaggerates as artists exaggerate – on stormy seas, *"he
	meant to pass them by."*
To disillusioned followers, *"he **acted** as if he were going further."*
"The whole city went out to hear him." Did it?
"If your right hand offends you, cut it off." Surely not!
All bluff and divine deceit, pretending secretly what he planned openly, making himself
	immortal when acting ridiculous.

Humour dressed in gravity and dignity, rarely depicted as joyful yet alive among
	experience, pleasure is scooped from natural things.
Dismissive of "touch not," "taste not" and "handle not," joking earnestly, he strides into
	excitements of seeing, hearing, tasting, smelling, touching, every experience
	beyond regret, each sensation priceless for the vigour they contain.
*"Behold, I make all things **new**"* – his finger ever on the pulse of every day.
Would he throw his head back to laugh at the moon and smile at the stars?
Careless as windflowers, beyond custom and regularity, exploring, reflecting, widening
	minds to atrocious pleasures and wildest possibilities, for him, experience more
	than belief, nothing so sensual as God that symphony of senses – all-seeing,
	all-hearing, all-tasting, all-feeling, all-smelling.

Humanness fusing with divinity among cups and saucers, the ploddingly dull and
	inflexibly mundane, he's felt vitality, emotional sincerity and instinct more than
	obligation.
Composer married to his music, moody poet more lyrical than libraries of law, feely man
	of pleasing melancholy and wistful sadness, of glances, stares, gestures and
	aroused atmospheres, makes him a person of pleasure not a source of safety
	and security.
Debonair sensualist, salvager of anticipations, flickers of mischief in his eyes, he resists
	narrowing himself to accepted practises, every enthusiasm dismissed by
	temple tradition.
Kicking-off shoes to the glamour of new mornings, rejecting dogma for sight and feeling,
	dismissing rites for countryside and seashore, he's carefree without loss of
	integrity.
No abstract theology but walking phantasmagoria of light, colour, odour and taste.
Joining the non-religious in a room, both would feel relaxed, no demand to bow down
	but invitations to sit beside.

EARNEST JOY OF FEELINGS

Why reject emotions and extoll reasoning, all I feel being more important than what I think?

Shudders of pleasure and feelings truest replicas of spiritual life, God stimulating the senses through things seen and felt.

If it feels wonderful, it is wonderful, the best philosophy permitting me to feel, understanding without sensation a poor apology.

If we interpret the letter, we must interpret the feelings – less logic, more sensations, ideas not embedded in emotions rarely coming to anything, both travelling hand in hand, neither pursued unless first attracted and none denied when they unexpectedly arrive.

Not searching for feelings but letting them find us, interpreting ourselves through experience in everything they suggest,

Each moment savoured attractions with given meanings, understanding that must be seen, touched, eaten and drank – withdrawing from them as unbalanced as over-indulging them.

Grasping meanings of life now and to come, we greedily see, hear, feel and taste voluptuous nectars of existence.

Divinity encountered in the sensuous – God feeling in us, we feeling in him, morality and enjoyment become identical.

Soul not divided from senses, natural coupled to spiritual, seeing, hearing, touching, tasting and smelling – *Deity* writing itself into strange dreams, primitive feelings and strange sensations wiser than ourselves, every experience the husk inside which celestial seeds ripen.

Emotions must be honoured, each feeling colours on a palette, the *Artist* mixing them into schemes not understood.

No sensation regimented, nothing predictable but priceless and breathless – lives changed more by pleasure than pain.

Transcendent emotions like clay waiting to be moulded, paint anticipating application, the musician feeling the strings, the sculptor caressing the stone – *"spies of the brain,"* chaffed Avicenna the Sufi, *"without which we disappear."*

Conscience the compass for our responses, a needle pointing to all we run away from and who we run to.

Emotion without coercion, impulses screaming suggestions heard and afterwards examined, breezy feelings touching everything that touches us.

Libraries of sensations, infectious for the energy they contain and God persuasive to be known.

A letting go to spontaneity, a jollying along in *'now-ness'* of things, prizing their uniqueness because of their transience, for refusing to *feel* our beliefs restricts their instructions – no feelings no meanings.

If dogma were subordinate to experience, there would be no dogma and *"Where there's no sincerity no emotion, and no dull person can be sincere."* 1.

Religious laws rejected for feelings, loveliness sensed in ordinary-ness, his moods rooted in skin more than textual knowledge and waist high in wonder, was there ever enough?

Felt emotions beyond sensible inducements, never striving to be other than who he was, he's looker and listener in pleasure, gentle melancholy and happy solemnity.

FRONTIERS OF SENSATION

Sensation lover, receptive to young surprise and felt mystery, emotion excelled scholarship and beauty aroused delight.
Pardoned from boredom, he freed feelings and dampened sectarian insistence, every sensed grandeur igniting wonder defying explanation.
Mid terrorising fatalities, life is devoured in deserving effusiveness with little loss when he's close-by, smiling, joking and sorrowing, his highest feelings bending to pleasure and pain.
Dipping imaginative brushes into pigments of reality, spent moments became alive in the smelt and seen.
Appetite and movement, arriving, receding – a goblet of wine, the touch of a hand, scented oil from a 'sinning' woman, body and soul welded into one, nothing standing still, every emotion hitched to tantalising 'otherness,' touching, loving and other tactile sensations hollering, *"I feel therefore I am."*

DISMISSAL OF FAITH

Thomas the Questioner not doubter – feelings in advance of thoughts, risking the consequences and practising faith without believing in it, he immerses himself in doubt, feelings less illusory than faith, doubts indicative of concern, a sense of certainty highly misleading.
Touching his Master's wound was phenomena to be snatched at.
Little patience with trusting without seeing, imagined faith frequently ending in betrayal.
If beauty and tenderness is glimpsed, faith becomes superfluous.
Enough intelligence to doubt, Thomas must thrust his hand beneath the chicken to feel the warmth of the egg.
I too must *touch* and *feel* – never forced into believing all I cannot sense and never clinging to creeds I have little interest in.
Excited by doubts as well as certainties, choices to believe or not believe, I resort to glad excess of unexpected delights, faith not rooted in emotion hardly coming to life, easily diluted to formula instead of instinct, to bargaining more than abandonment, precise reasoning instead of effort-less emotion.
Like love defying reason, experience reaches deeper than belief.
Maybe we need challenging by riotous doubt more than presumptuous belief, the liberator called doubt always receiving warmest welcomes.
As for *"faith to move mountains,"* too noisy, reckless and theatrical!
Pride refuses to doubt and only dull people never question all they are told.
Better honest doubt than arrogant faith arousing over-confidence and superiority.
No warnings to believe but sensitivity to feelings yielding similar results, experience surpassing knowledge, feely fingers thrust into sights and sounds, only then can I believe the unbelievable.

If I'm wrong, I'm relieved in my wrongness.
If I don't know where truth is, at least I know where it isn't, mistaken ideas never
  interfering with happy inspiration and doubt no obstacle to sincerity.
*"We have **seen** him with our eyes, we have **touched** him with our hands"* – better felt
  than lectured, religion purged of forceful faith becoming a sunny hope-full thing.

DELICATE IMPRESSIONS AND THOUGHTFUL EMOTIONS

In Simon's house, everyone ignored sensations.
Hands and blistered feet plunged in cold water, singing kisses on weathered cheeks,
  scented oil on raven hair, everything pleasurable when you know they have
  endings.
Longings bounced around the room: *"Be generous,"* he twittered. *"Deluge me with
  extravagance. Poor people will fidget you forever. I won't."*
If feelings are language, there must be expression.
Shaping us we listen, every sensation obeying invisible designs.
Like him, exiled to earth experiencing giddy emotions, every gasp of pleasure disturbing
  lights of distant Pleiades.
A free-spirited letting go, a gifting to 'waste' time, seductive intensities prompting choice
  not compulsion.
Mundane mingling with sacred, incidentals immersed in numinosity, light-heartedness
  never without substance and highest wisdom resulting from cheerfulness.
No kindness performed without sentiment, ethics crass without frolic, and who needs
  timid faith in saturated moments?
Oh dear!
Trying to believe is so difficult, obscure faith hard going, pursuing perfection irritatingly
  impossible and with all our believing, something escapes us.
Authority relaxed, heads crowded with songs, feel-able, he sneaks into humanness
  never begging, *"Forgive us our happiness."*

BEWITCHMENT OF EYESIGHT

Man of "many looks" no moralist blind to people and beauty, but observer, everything
  sighted warming him Godward.
Unlike ourselves observing only what we want to see, he's a magnifying glass helping
  us contemplate all we see but never notice.
Attentive to the obvious, snatching at everything perceived, listening eyes marvel and
  admire, "Observation the key to knowledge," clamoured de Vinci.
Gazing round the gallery he's lost in the paintings, everything beautiful arousing
  welcomes, nature the mother of sensuality reflecting divine imagination.
Prostrate in long grass, the looker stamps his image on all he looks at, imperishable
  beauty pressing through the pores of his skin – everything expressing *Deity,*
Wisdom born of sight and wonder, physical reflecting spiritual, he's the talking eyes of a
  friend not a stranger.

"Consider the lilies." He looks and looks again, seeing something inside as well as outside himself.
Idealising the ordinary it becomes an idyll, artist, poet pointing to grandeur in ordinariness prompting listener response of, *"Why didn't I notice that before?"*
With perceptive sight and feelings aroused, every object seen and felt a window reflecting worlds within and without.
Seized by sentiments more than analyses, sensory arouses imagination in winding
    elegance of Jordan and stars yearning earthward,
    a lonely shepherd leaning on his crook,
    milky eyed doves and argumentative sparrows,
    composed meadows and golden corn hurrying skywards,
    fun of sycamore seeds spinning to earth,
    dips and curves of open roads unfolding before him,
    inner beauty of human faces, painful mystery in human eyes and
    countless other images carelessly unrecorded –
A creeping sensuality, a theophany of beauty.
Virtues alive in passions, *Experimentalist* and *Adventurer* is freed from temple constraint to easy astonishment.

"Happy are the clean in heart for they shall **see** *God,"* an *otherness* in everything.
Who on earth has said that before?
It's a gift of enchantment worth handing down.
"If you want to live in other presences, come and see!"
Seeing is knowing, to know is to see – the *"pure in heart* **see** *God,"* scriptures silently spoken in skies, texts in stars, manuscripts in mountains and old stones, truth among dirt and dishevelment, innocence and ignorance in eyes looking and pleading.
Beyond the obvious, hushed identities hiding far and near, every exhilaration beyond emotional indulgence or merrily producing it.
Reckless beauty prompting 'oohs' and 'ahs,' exquisite wonders never satisfying thrills they arouse, *Seeker of Astonishment* scatters emotions like broken colours in spilt petrol.
Inebriated by pink mornings, golden noon and blue evenings, he quaffs life's wine mature and undiluted.

THE DELECTABLE AND AWKWARD

Feelings curdle into pleasures at dandle of babies, winds clutched in outspread arms, aloneness in the rain, and nudity of water on sunburnt skin.
Crisp sand and cool grass squeeze between bare toes, silver fish slither through grasping fingers.
Casual among lookers and listeners, a friend's head nestles pleasingly on his shoulder.
Void of thoughtless indifference, he feels for hungry sparrows, the donkey dragging a cart, a dying dog in the gutter.
Alive among rough and smooth, delicate in touch and discriminate of eye, he enjoys himself till it hurts.

With bewildered smiles he attracts femininity, especially Magdala woman.
Chastity not contradicting pleasure, things used as allurement to men erupt in respect for him, perfume, kisses and falling hair – languorous sentiments of awkward sensuality.

HOLY RECKLESSNESS OF IMBIBING

Food for thought!
Possessing gifts of pleasure as well as sorrows, *"The Son of Man came **eating** and **drinking**"* on everybody's behalf.
Washing religion from hands and face, the speaking tongue tastes, pleasure needing no apology,
God crowing *"Good!"* over everything created as gazes swung from glories in the sky to glories on the table.
Sight transformed to savour, he's taster – material penetrating spiritual.
"Him verily seeing and fully feeling. Him spiritually hearing and then delectably smelling and sweetly swallowing," chattered 14th century Julian of Norwich.
Wisdom in tasting, pleasure in expectation, the palate no less than eye or ear.
"O taste and see that God is good," tasting him in the knowledge he reveals.
"Whether you eat or drink … do it for the glory of God."
"The fragrance of those desirable meats." 2,
Spilling wines of proximity, every flavour insinuating itself, like Aphrodite he pours wine mixed with nectar, mind and body nudged to thankfulness and satisfaction.

Leaping from the dish, tables of longing are never left bare.
"Enjoy yourself! Sip the honey and you'll covet the comb."
A secular spirituality savouring desire, the tyranny of food refreshing and worshipful, teeth and tongue welcomed without remorse.
Eating being intimate union, *"He made us to **want** that like gods we might be **satisfied**,"* effused Thomas Traherne shredding beef on bread. Drooling sensations of flavours, culinary pleasures of the 'forbidden' and every *"tyranny of the palate."* 3.
When opportunities arrived, *"he made them sit at the table and waited on them."*
"Brought to the banqueting house," tasty luxuries served for the pleasure of every guest.

Grabbing enjoyment in horrors of extravagance, sensualist wrestles with moralist among banner-waving accusations: *"Glutton! Wine drinker! Beauty out! Sensuality out!"*
Relishing life to proportions of poorness, he has everything he needs.
Never patronising the poor or living fat among much and nothing, *"Love,"* pattered Plato, *"being child of poverty and plenty."*
Dashing to the kitchen ignoring food laws of his day, he *"Spreads a table before me …"* smacking lips, licking fingers, wallowing with thankfulness and pleasure, eating heartily but always ready to share.
What a party we could stage for him, his eagerness surpassing wildest satisfaction!

Saliva dribbling down chin, author of Ecclesiastes shrieks, *"There is nothing better for a man than that he should eat and drink, and that he should make his soul enjoy good in his labour. This also I saw, **that it was from the hand of God.**"*

Spouting huge jokes on himself he snaps, *"John the Baptist went without food. He never touched a drop of wine and you said, 'He must be crazy.' But I eat my food and drink my wine and you say, 'What a glutton Jesus is. And he drinks! And has the lowest sort of friends."*
Prolonged fasting produces diminished sensibility.
No fasting for him – it's hungry work!
Jollifying moments to be enjoyed rather than extracting spiritual lessons, celebrants flop reddest wine into spacious cups – tasting becoming knowing: *"When I'm eating I know nothing, when I've finished, I understand."* 4.
Beverage for the body, gobbets for the soul – a unity of being, food and eater becoming one, crunching and chewing acts of homage, helpings of proportion celebrating thankfulness for simple things.
"He who tastes not, knows not," slurped Rumi, taste God-given for our enjoyment for why should delicacies be delicious if we were meant to decline them?
Everything aligns to *eternal love,* God feeding on our pleasures, nothing inherently unholy.
Sacraments of divinity in pleasure loving people, *"**feasting** on the **abundance** of your house you give them drink from rivers of delights,"* respond hungry people knowing the happiness of food.
Every morsel dunked in humanness understood by those who experience,
"sausage out of which the garlic sang,
some cheese which laid down and cried
a long-necked flask containing bottled sunshine." 5.
No conscientious gruel but dancing girls of joy and cheer, *Song-giver* alive in gulps of surprise and bites of mercy.
God's mouth dripping recipes in spendthrift celebrations of life at that *"Covenant of the table."* 6.
While desires prove we need, body bows to conscience.
"Tell me what you like and I'll tell you who you are," 7. so why hug menus when meals can be devoured?
Not only what we eat but the spirit in which we eat it, idling as we do at groaning tables spread with delight, loss of reputation and sporadic folly imperative to happy, humble repentance!

Would he repent of epicurean extravaganzas and gastronomic flirtations?
Probably not – commitment to causes not easy on empty stomachs.
Was he doused in guilt after eruptions of hunger or, *"Let's eat and make merry,"* in transgressive quests for pleasure?
Give him credit, we all crave escape from drabness and boredom:
Like myself reposed with book, promiscuous chocolate and lighted pipe – everyone needing pleasure from some stimulant, all of us permitted two or three

weaknesses, most of us secretly aspiring for something naughty – dashes of scandal surpassing smug self-righteousness.

Thinking of himself, in insane generosity he thinks of others.
Aware that eating is *Kindly Light's* sandwich for sadness and ancient cure for ennui,
    "My cup runneth over."
    "My cup that makes me drunk, how goodly it is," sniggers the Latin Vulgate.
If so, *"Everyone should eat, drink and **enjoy** the good of all their labour, it is the gift of God."*
Practical helpings of perfection plumped into well-being, the constant feast of conversation, wine of celebrants perfumed with *God's* humanness, *"Deity,"* mused mystic Eckhart, being *"scrumptious and delicious."*
Prodigal boy dawdles home to feasting not rejection and, *"they all began to have a **wonderful time**."*
Uninvited guest at every banquet, no morbid fasting subtracting delight and happiness, but goodness in talking and hugging,
Like people at a party – eating and drinking fighting doldrum and dullness: *"Eat that which is good and let your soul delight itself in fatness"* and afterwards sleepy contentment.
"To constitute a feast," whooped Patmore, *"there must be **much more than enough**,"*
Sanctified by love and reverence, feelings expanding beyond cramped horizons, the soul is raised to higher aims and finer achievements.
Famed wine-taster makes him *"Master of the spiritual drinking feast,"* 8. each swig freeing throats to melody and mirth, prophet fading into infinity, celebrant springing into song:
    "As for that which is forbidden,
    Whatever could be dafter?
    A thing banned in this world,
    Yet abounds in the hereafter." 9.
Spurts of grape juice throbbing with summer, apricots swollen with sweetness, running water cold and dark, olives rolling in oil, honey gluey and golden – each lick sunlight and desire appetisingly eternal, every sentiment celebrating *Infinity* alive in everything, *"Our God great and the cook his prophet."* 10.
One to be listened to as simplicities erupt into experience, voracious faith into feelings, law into poetry, austerity into desire.
But no happiness without pain.
Feelings wearing away in efforts to sustain them, a final supper sadness.
Bread soaked in darkness, cup lifted to lips, yellow wine spiked with poison, he swigs its pointless misery.
Like ourselves, intensities like water slip through cupped hands, everything craved not guaranteed to receive, all hoped for may not happen, objects reached after not always obtainable.

                                                CRESCENDOS OF HEARING

As in a shell, dwells sighing seas, sounds sculpture into words.

Thoughtfully silent, he bends an ear to sounds of the deep earth.
Eavesdropping, *Perceptive Listener* hears melancholy voices baying from crowds,
> gusts of wind like lost tunes,
> old songs of beautiful sorrow subduing anger and fear,
> sparrows bickering on roof tops,
> weathered voices of friends and followers and
> the speaking heart of nature as in olden days when stones shouted for recognition, trees whispered profundities and angels talked to humans.

Surely, like ourselves, he's drawn to music, no culture void of song and dance – drifting harmonies speaking felt things beyond understanding and soaring rhythms arousing gusto and madness.

Unlike people never hearing trains when residing near railway stations, he has an inner ear for human needs.

From indwelling silence, the wailing poor more penetrating than thunder of worlds through space, cats shrieking on rooftops, and bitchy religion like lightning strikes booming: *"Believe this!" "Accept this!"*

AROMAS AND MEMORY

Not forgetting languages of smells, that short-cut to recollections; between nostalgia and anticipation, far-off impressions evoking the senses.

Possessing smelling ability of a realist, aromas arouse the persuasive and obscure, everyone leaving vapour trails shifty and inspiring, each scenting their vices as animals sniff approaching storms.

For him, like ourselves, every smell connected to experience.

Undertones of disembodied days, vignettes of sensations from faraway, lazy odours of wine the colour of topaz, familiar smell of clothes, temple smells, pomegranate smells, sickness, misery and death smells.

The sorrowing nostalgia of mother's baked bread, every mouthful tasting of love, *"Smell and taste,"* scribbled Proust, *"poised a long time like souls ready to remind us."*

Bouquets of childhood mornings lost among measureless distances, lighted windows at dusk and ageless emotion on time-etched faces.

Tearful reminders that once away there's no return, the throb of life lost in efforts to retain, every memory suggesting somewhere fingers cannot point to.

Throbbing with suggestions that agonise angels, overpowering perfumes of passing women, shocking and moody, drenching odours of lilies reeking spells and early morning hay stooks in mangled sunshine,

Every odour evoking responses like relaxation of lavender, sexual attraction of musk, happiness of bananas, comfort of spikenard and other fragrances too cunning to analyse.

Soul of Thought and Feeling – quintessence of sensuality, animated by sight, sound, touch, taste and smells, emotions teasing thought, arousing smiles and tears igniting gratitude in one who never demanded pleading prayers and ingratiating worship.

Ourselves like him, in emotive oscillations more persuasive than statements, in hand clasps, hugs and ramping exaltations of touch and hesitation.

EXCLAMATIONS OF THE POET

*"My yoke is **easy** and my burden **light**,"* he says in chatty style.
Springy *lightness*, puffs of magic, pleasure as well as endurance opposing unflagging cross-carrying undervaluing promised joys.
"You are not seeing straight brother James," decrees the Gnostic gospel, Acts of John.
*"Do you not see the man standing there who is handsome fair and **cheerful looking.**"*
Speaking joy, had he done so with serious expression friends would tease, *"We never saw it Jesus. It's ages since you smiled. Explain what you mean!"*
Gluttons are never glum, wine tasters frequently uproarious, prompting awareness of prophets of misery and dictators who rarely laugh.

Whimsy and imagination spring from this non-Christian man, *"A leader of such men who receive the truth with **pleasure**,"* quipped historian Josephus.
Pleasure beyond labour, nonsense a lifesaver, reality surpassing common sense.
Important trivialities arousing laughter, pleasing the simple, annoying the traditional,
"Serious things never understood without humorous things," trilled Plato.
No disciplined obedience but ferocious thankfulness, invitations to parties not seminars where *"good measures are pressed down, shaken together and spill over the top."*
No subjection to petty rules, moral warnings and 'truths' one can't believe when failing to confirm felt experience.

Why demonise sensuality?
God gladly embraced in feelings and conscience in contrast to narrow-minded religions dismissing cries of helpless happiness, people hurting each other more through austerity than enjoyment.
Nothing restrictive, nothing intimidating but everyone welcomed into eyes reflecting suggestions strange and timeless, his living words persuasively simple.
I hear a ringing voice offering courage of opportunities.
He's introducing a revolutionary way of seeing, thinking and behaving during our stay on earth: *"Just be kind and patient. Forgive people like you forgive yourself. Show mercy. Try and live in peace not war. Seek goodness and purity. Be thankful, stay humble, courteous and unpretentious, then you'll be **happy!**"*
Making sense of everything, he thinks lightly yet seriously.
No efforts to believe, crushing laws or threatened punishments, but simple affection, quiet sympathy and leisurely acts of kindness in thinking behaviour that insinuates itself like photographs, wistful music, sunsets or the beauty of a woman.
Such wisdom whistles for silence and makes me religiously forgetful!
Among adorable errors and exquisite failures, **everyone** aiming at their best, every desire to be better indicative of progress.

Delighting in *Creator*, chasing amusements as far as possible, none of which are sensible, his feelings sturdy enough to grind pebbles to powder in contrast to dogmas of his day making matters of greatest importance least exciting.
So why repent of enjoyment, life without pleasures being half a life?
Risks exist, but what is life without risks?
Every euphoria a premonition of dawn after dark, good cheating evil and *Himself,* speaking fingers rapping closed doors twittering, *"How **you** see me determines who **you** are."*

LIGHT ON THE FAR SIDE OF THE HILL

"Take up your cross and follow me."
Believing it but not knowing how to carry it, every criss-cross experience restraining and releasing freeing imperfect understanding from invented burdens and not-needed self-cursing – no one living by sobriety alone.
Enamoured as we are by self-pity, self-esteem and self-righteous denial of all we are fond of, better making light of ourselves than chasing the unattainable, living carelessly in light than bemoaning darkness,
More *"hey-ho melancholy,"* 11. *God* crucifying in the "dark night of the soul," loss of faith, grief, guilt and despair, *"the whole creation groaning and travailing together in pain,"* but also chewing cud of scrumptious sensations.
Heroic sanctity teasing wild emotions, happiness and hardship harmonising each other and crucifixion never lasting a lifetime.
*"Happy are you who weep now, **for you will laugh**,"* laughter illuminating darkest moments.
Tensions of opposites producing balance, his crosses double-faced coins spun dizzily into the inevitable, despair one side, exhilaration the other, two talismans of disturbance and delight, agony and consolation.
Enjoyment of dreams but having to wake up, a sword piercing the soul but hissing glasses inspiring giddy feet – opposing enigmas, one never clouding the other, in contrast to becoming *"cross with our crosses,"* 12. making them intrusive to carry.

Irrepressible longings labelled sinful?
Stress laid on sorrow and sacrifice, whine and woe?
Humble seriousness never helps people to feel less wretched so why this stripping of "self" and sacrificing to "him," guilt made to look virtuous, self-mistrust diminishing uniqueness and morbid submission producing distortion instead of completeness.
"What I do is me: for that I came." 13. A cat remains a cat, a dog remains a dog, a human a human, nobody ever "dying to self," every individual developing its own uniqueness, shaped as we are for mercy and affection.
Straining after light results in exhaustion, our follies mud on skin not disease in bloodstream, *Grand Companion* pleased with the little we do while aware of the little we have, our questionable qualities not failures to extinguish but eminence of who we are.

Risking follies of independence, I cannot slavishly worship deity, in desperate but sincere moments dismissing a sense of responsibility and taking God for granted.

In faithful betrayal, fighting him becomes a way of remaining honest with him, for if we hate ourselves, we'll hate everybody – *"Blessed are they who heal us of our self-despising,"* botheration and discomforts never articles of faith, our lives changed more by pleasure than pain, villainy than virtues.

Why be perfect? It sounds so dull, pleasure not self-denial being the essence of well-being.

Solemnity has its place, but religion mixed with worldly awareness are healthy combinations.

Attempting to avoid vice, we all have our little "vicelets" grizzled Dostoyevsky, everyone reaching for something better that they never attain, and everyone given to snippets of wickedness.

No belief need be sin-obsessed, constant repentance weighing heavier than the crime, over-much religion robbing humanness of its richness and many iniquities not iniquitous at all.

Joy is the elixir of life, pleasure a diagnostic aid tickling the soul, food, friends, family and lovers feelable eucharists reminding us to rely on instinct not dungeon sobriety – a yielding to endorphins, a refusal to be guilty about bliss and euphoria.

JOYFUL RECKLESSNESS

Everything making us feel good must be good, to delight in things is not mockery, nothing being unholy except our poisoning of others and souring thickest cream inside ourselves.

More demanding than self-denial is enjoyment, gloomier than happiness is rigorous self-condemnation and more complex than chastened resignation, dancing to the music of our days. *"Come unto me all that labour and are heavy-laden and I will refresh you."* Heavy-laden not a requirement but a release!

Swamping banks of exclusive beliefs, *Galilean Poet* brings youth to the world, his overwrought voice hollering, *"Truth shall make you **free**!"*

*"**My joy** I leave with you!"* – wandering, sensuous joy never translated into discussion.

*"A great **joy** came upon us and a peaceful **care-freeness** like our Lord*," observed an early gnostic writer, 14.

His *"glad tidings"* better sung in meadows than rigid systems, poetic persuasions more than intense rules, windows of surprise more than Gates of Wailing, his numerous sentiments never commanding us to 'behave' but be real.

AN INVITATION TO PANDEOMIUM

*"Did not our hearts **burn** within us?"* prattled listless travellers.
Of course! **Feeling** one's beliefs expands astonishment.
Jauntiness pointing to hope, not a planet exploding in doom but awe and wonder.

An ordination into priests of pleasure, a holy hedonism, cheeky heresy and celestial narcissism to cliff-edge dissipation without dishonour, qualities touched, felt and dripping like rubies into wine.
Jamborees of sight, palate, hearing and aroma invading flattened passions and chastised senses.
Warmth in things touched and touching us, thankfully invoking suspicions of a *Smiling Consoler* shouldering poverty, arousing mirth and laughing in the dark.
Emotional ingredients making us greater than splendours of who we are, our lives birthed to intoxication as well as age.
A marvellous outrageousness and shocking provocation diminishing institutions governed by an angry God, no religion lasting that forbids pleasure among its people.

1. William Hale White.
2. St. Augustine.
3. Zola.
4. A. A. Gill.
5. Kenneth Grahame (Wind in the Willows).
6. John Ruskin.
7. Philo.
8. Don Quixote.
9. Abu Nuwas (poem. The Wine in Heaven).
10 Jerome K. Jerome.
11 Stevie Smith.
12 Evelyn Underhill.
13 Gerard Manley Hopkins.
14 The Acts of Peter and the Twelve.

FOOLISHNESS

Not all people, but certainly some people, live curiously fated lives, in which they seemed doomed to carry out actions which bear no relationship to ordinary probability, and are dictated by necessities which have nothing to do with common sense.
Robertson Davies

Sense and nobleness it seems to me to go mad for the beautiful Messiah. It seems to me great wisdom in a man if he wishes to go mad for God; In Paris there has never been seen such great philosophy as this. Whoever goes mad for Christ certainly seems afflicted and in tribulation; but he is an exalted master of nature and theology. Whoever goes mad for Christ certainly seems crazy to people. It seems he is off the road to anyone without experience of the state. Whoever wishes to enter this school will discover new learning. He who has not experienced madness does not yet know what it is.
Jacapone de Todi (13th cent)

If any of you thinks he is wise by the standards of this age, he should become a fool so that he may become wise. For the wisdom of this world is foolishness in God's sight.
1 Corinthians 3:18

Even in the smallest group only that is acceptable which is accepted by the majority, it must be accepted with resignation. But resignation alone is not enough. On the contrary, resignation encourages self-doubt from which an isolated individual who has to stand for something, will in certain circumstances suffer severely.
C. G. Jung

Critical turning-points in history tend to occur, we are told, when a form of life and its institutions are increasingly felt to cramp and obstruct the most vigorous productive forces …
Isaiah Berlin

The wisest person of all, the way I see it, is the one who calls himself a fool at least once a month.
Dostoevsky. Bobok

Enflamed with love it was his great desire to sing, contemplate, ponder and admire.
Thomas Traherne

FOOLISHNESS

We all gaze at different horizons, I at my level, others at theirs. Closer he's presumed, more his breath is felt on one's cheek. Too close and he's fuzzy, confusing and complicated, but re-invented. He slips into personal experience like cosy shoes.

WISDOM OF THE CLOWN

On heels of sublimity shuffles wisdom in foolishness and carnivalesque in the strangely serious.

Peasant teacher and homeless vagrant clad in anybody's clothes, Compo king in woolly hat and dogged persistency, Charlie Chaplin in baggy trousers, crushed hat and tatty boots.

Derisory yet sincere, lethal and absurd, dismissing reputation to extreme limits, he places himself in touching distance of imbeciles.

Folly is deified in Cervantes' Knight astride a nag, failing underdog becoming hero in tragic comedy.

Fusions of piety and carnival in Dostoyevsky's "Idiot" laughing at himself, the most innocent the most mocked, befriended and betrayed by his friends.

Announcing different ideas he was thought peculiar, an expected person who didn't come as expected, the dead-beat maverick winning by losing.

A wandering prophet with begging bowl, no reputation to protect; a buck-carrier deserving a stallion but loaned a mule, making children shout and cynics jeer.

Hero becomes fool in a throw-away figure of stupid goodness, daring honesty and amusement of being misunderstood.

Forgiving the unforgiveable, looks conveying as much as speech, in mock solemnity he launches into inspired lunacy. Embracing foolishness, he knows that freedom is too precious to remain in the hands of the pompous and powerful.

Loathing decorum and authority, more talk than punishment and giving other than requested in dreadful strengths of daftness, his unpredictability and disturbing inspiration nudges friends and followers into all kinds of adventures.

Never malicious, *Wise Jester* rattling his bells, gives support to victims of intolerant religion, his humorous irreverence violating sacred law; everything spoken scoffed at until it becomes worth listening to.

Like wind, *"blowing where it wills,"* zest of Seers dashes through his veins, force tinged with frailty, wit and wisdom mixed with folly, tragedy with absurdity in victim of sublime sincerity preferring to be wrong than orthodox.

Poet dreamer of flashing eyes and tangled gypsy locks.

Anarchic clown of fun in melancholy and excitements of lawless living.

God's Harlequin getting himself into trouble and wriggling his way out.

Troubadour, vagabond, rebuffed knight and wounded lover with rainbow scarf and battered violin, strolling from town to town, his lyrical stories dazzling city and village.
Reverently eccentric, pioneer in folly, rags of respectability hurled aside, he's courageous enough to be beggar, bold enough to become vagabond, an anti-social dubbed with dementia by Gentile, Jew and icy tacticians opposing change – fools and heretics forever wielding romantic appeal.
Unlearning everybody, religion is reduced to unreliable ideas and outlines gone wrong.
Complex not stupid, hidden truths translate to trivialities of everyday language, nuisance as well as innovator his friendliness always slightly menacing.
Theology is mortified, family offended, friends disappointed and society astounded, but no originality without risk, if he wasn't free, he'd be drab and forgotten.

Donkey-riding, *Infinity's* young fool, lopes triumphantly across sensibility making the pious less appealing and boredom less bearable.
Ignoring reputation he embraces disgrace and shame.
Professional in foolishness, he's eternity's archetype for useless people, wild, scornful, sporty, possessing the wisdom of fools and foolishness of wisdom, secret meanings lurking in the logically ridiculous.
No purple vesture but derisory monarch of verminous rags and walking stick sceptre.
Jewish Jester, sawdust carpenter see-sawing between splendour and ridicule.
Nerdy in common clothes, avoiding respectable appearances, he hovers between wisest prophet and Balaam's talking ass.

SOPHISTICATED DESPISERS

Killed midst garbled shouts, weathered words spangle battered brow, *"He saved others but can't save himself,"* comic and tragic converge in life's saddest joke – birthed as king, ending as dupe, 1. but by nonsense and failure the *"kingdom of God arrives among us."*
Laughter and tears, comedy and tragedy swap seats – from innocent lamb to dumb sheep, he's set-up to be silly by the daftness of his flock.
An ugly duckling destined for swan-hood yet laughing-stock of the duck pond.
A non-violent anarchist tilting windmills in imaginative extravagance.
Faultless fool mocked but not ignored and donkey-like needing to be muzzled and tamed, but better buffoonery than idealism wrapped in narrowness, or blinded strength of the strong seeing no needs but their own.
Absurdity and poignancy conjoin in thud of boards, clang of nails, descent into darkness and futility lingering in sighs.
Doom-drenched fool and upside-down hero willing to be wounded – gobs of spit, wretchedness of matted hair, nerves twitching, breathless, thirsty and nailed high amid infuriating flies.
Deafening shouts from gallery as love looms pathetic, mercy nonsensical, compassion ineffectual.
The less they know, more they ridicule.
"Stone him!" "Crucify him!" but the cat slips through the hatch.

He can't die yet – foolishness monopolises his message, written off as farcicality misses surpassing inspiration.
Before such lunacy, minds sink power-less as nonsense excels, anyone claiming a message becoming a risk, their many contradictions sourced in wisdom, their discretion discarded for devotion, their ambiguities pointing to clarities.
It's *Way Shower's* trickster game then and now, failures proving we're worth testing, plans fulfilling themselves without our awareness.

No one can play the fool like he played the fool, or step from the sublime to the ridiculous.
Defying explanation, from tragic to playful, *Beggar-boy* becomes king quitting rules to follow futility stretching logic beyond limits.
Spinning myths and love stories, he's compelled to perform!
And perform he did, changing dull repetitions to dripping colours too bright to see.
Foolishly disguised he encouraged instead of leading, entertained by adjusting affections and provoked to new thinking, his shrewdness always helping him to pretend.

Risking absurdity, gazing rather than blinking, he perceives infinity in shrieking winds, sublimity in sparrows, deity in bread crusts and visionaries in simpletons.
Patron saint of misfits in *"decorum of stupidity,"* 2. ill at ease among staunch believers, an unfamiliar spectacle attracts fools and fantasists.
"Who's the more foolish," twittered Obi-Wan Kenobi, *"the fool, or the fool who follows him?"*
Life and religion being sad fun and non-stop comedy, everyone enjoying circus moments in epic spiritual quests.
More funny repartee than finger wagging, preparing to leap, he steps back for a run,
Reminding everyone they live on edges of becoming as well as departing,
    none falling from acceptance, everyone irreplaceable,
    nobody breaking laws but laws breaking them and
    the holiest tumbling distance from the gutter.
We can only greet this jester speechless and bewildered!

JESTERS AND PROPHETS

Earth rolls into Winter and eagerly into Spring.
He the prototype, historical fools the copies.
Fumbling souls, *"not normal people, nor sensible like you and me,"* 3. but blunderers rushing in where theologians fear to tread.
Shabby, clumsy kids in rooms packed with chinaware, earnest plodders coming, going and disagreeing.
The supernaturally gawkish nailing down tarpaulin in monstrous winds, swinging golf clubs in electric storms, stomping toward execution humming old-fashioned hymns.
Seers of detached understanding, smouldering enthusiasm and reverent stupidity speaking sensible nonsense.

Imagined heretics, prisoners of odd ideas reaching for the moon, stepping off precipices
without looking and treading tightropes in wild abandonment.
A rag-tag rabble to laugh at so that *Unnameable* can be seen, like their mentor, taking
risks, flopping, failing and bouncing back.

THE FREEDOM OF STRANGENESS

Immersed in gifts of silliness, their earnestness makes them awkward.
We've read of them and encountered them in religion, politics and **each other!**
Fairground buffoons in exaggerated humility, mass-produced sanctity and monumental
hypocrisy, reputation and beliefs being taken far too seriously.
In gaffes and idiocies, commanding and foretelling, kooky prophets of importance
making metaphysical trumpet calls; overheated worshippers and lovers of
causes straining vision to the intelligible.
Giddy risk takers, God's eschatological jokers opposed to prisoners of faith, their
sensible nonsense and instructive absurdities disturbing calm lives, smooth
running and balanced behaviour.
Messianic loonies and squinters at Doomsday Clocks, their formidable crankiness
peddling world-wide conspiracies and final curtain calls.
Happy bands of apocalyptic heroes, garrulous prophets and talented tub thumpers, their
prophetic impatience announcing wrath that never happens, looking for
kingdoms always coming but never arriving, catastrophes suddenly cancelled
and Armageddon shelved.
What's holding things up?
The end hasn't come but warnings abound.
Clocks strike twelve, the world carries on and obstinate *Messiah* refuses to return.
Holy quirkiness swamping sensitivity, lines are thin between pathetic and comical.
Don't they understand that events aren't worsening but aging, age producing frailty
carries wisdom!
With preposterous theories yelled effectively, leaps into clumsiness instead of evil,
accused of oddness they oblige by being so.
Flirting with the ludicrous, *Adviser to the Stupid* is pursued, visions waggishly failing as
they bumble along, different believers reacting in different ways, one person's
heresy another person's choice, making unity impossible.
"Christianity demands that you make a fool of yourself," quipped Richard Coles,
Each inspired duffer the irony of God, a manuscript of their *Maker* and slapstick
performer in comedies of religious fervour.
Dumbness becoming eloquence, Baldrick, Bean and Basil attract greatest applause,
inspiration not equalling their inclinations, their silliness appealing especially
when mistaken.

DEPTHS BEHIND APPEARANCES

Noble nuisances, free-lance Prophet figures, cunning in virtues, genius in neurosis,
inspirational in visionary extravagance, their mad pranks more interesting than

vulgarities of bumptious leaders, correctness of the self-satisfied and civilised warnings from the impressively pious.
A simpleton devotion in disruptive messages from rank outsiders, repetitive Sunday themes becoming a patchwork of dull conventionality.
Untutored in decorum, exemplary in innocence, ridiculous but never vicious, tactlessness serves at the altar, nurses instructing doctors, the child going to work, the parent returning to school, each imaginative fool prepared to be useless for God and in doing so, snatching ascendency over the convinced and professional.

Be patient, let them be!
Aren't we all mixtures of strength and nonsense, moderation and extravagance?
When everybody is a fool, we are unable to know a fool.
Fools must perform vague purposes, wonders dwelling deep within where nobody thinks of looking.
None can be ignored any more than trees blow down in gales.
Prophets of doom being guides pointing to happier times, their craziness redeeming us all.
Critique may be disguised wisdom, truth alive in the banal as well as the programmed.
Like *him*, better foolishness than tyranny.
How dreary if there was no stupidity or God-given peculiarities, the holiest hiding skeletons in cupboards, fools flaunting them in public.
Embracing inconsistencies, sincerity abounds, enthusiasm excusing uselessness resigning them to comfortable delusions, water seeking its own level, long-buried seeds germinating into unfamiliar flowers.
Better quagmire paths than no path at all, bold imprudence than drabness, marvellous ignorance than monochrome teachers of common sense.
If *Existent One* spouts through donkey teeth, he speaks through fools, stupidity "tails" side of the coin in blundering wisdom, all snatching places in some wondrous plan and no one stopped from becoming an amateur.
To them, discretion is the enemy of devotion and disobedience expressions of freedom.
Inevitable mistakes become good mistakes, no reason or order but a synthesis of the two.

UNCERTAINTY OF ATTRACTION

Aware that religion possesses power to kill as well as enlighten, fools are informants of religious unreliability prompting awareness that we have all dug ourselves out of rubbish heaps and must never imagine we are holier than anyone else.
Seeing their foolishness is a revelation of our own, every utopia disgorging misfits, all beliefs possessing prophets of chaos.
End results matter, weakness creating less competition – more vulnerability, less betrayal.
God's wisdom in kindly vindictiveness and comedy, no one escaping who they are – here today, gone tomorrow, who is right, who is wrong? everyone yelling sense and contradiction to their coffin.

Dunce, predictor and prophetic scarecrow banished from our institutions?
Tolerance is needed with theories that sensible doctrine describes as absurd.
Only fools sees falsities in religion, the rest of us put up with it – religious laws so silly that silliness is the only response.
Without the idiot, silence reigns when shouts should be heard, seers, poets and holy idiots sighting simple truths wise ones miss.
Protecting faith from stagnation, extremity rails against extremity, sensible, qualified believers as un-hinged as holy fools.
Christianity has become too clever, protesting its rights when it has none, exclusive possessors of truth, merciless in moral edicts resulting in despotism – institutions diminishing in size when stable and uniform, adherents losing their individuality when pressed to follow others.

SACRED HERESY

While devotion fears disorder, the fool can't care a damn.
Outsiders must always have a place, cure their hysterics and they lose their virtues, written off robs their challenge to mediocrity,
Their many riddles solved through intuition more than analyses, less written words, more reading between lines, thoughts stated but not explained, everything ridiculous when no one reads another's soul.
Little honour earned in foolishness, but if crowds are to have fun, rules obeyed, truth protected and institutions respected, faces must be slapped and the buck passed.
More fractious the event, louder screams for scapegoats.
Heretics denounced, wisest clods mocked, like wasps, ridiculously small but annoyingly dangerous.
"You're different!
Something's wrong!
You're not like you used to be!
You've become a heretic!"
But following *Holy Outcast* generates castaways, erratic, cynical and misguided – wrongness and weakness becoming attributes, a saving sense of the ridiculous redeeming them all, their every comicality acted with sincerity and each stupidity subtle inspiration, *"making up whatever is lacking and remains to be completed in the afflictions of Jesus."*
Greater the struggle, greater the failure until failures become holy revelations, making victims right by their wrongs and wrong by their rights – everyone having fun in their faith rather than wrecked by it.

1. *Idea from Harvey Cox. The Feast of Fools.*
2. *Oliver Goldsmith.*
3. *Mark Lebanon.*

ANGER

When the mode of the music changes, the walls of the city shake.
Plato. Republic

… the moral is that the Christ of the gospel might actually seem more strange and terrible than the Christ of the Church.
G. K. Chesterton

And when he had looked around about on them in anger …
Mark 3:5

Far from being a sin, proper remonstration with God is the activity of a healthy faith relationship with him.
Leonard Pine

It is clear that only by expressing our anger and hatred directly to God will we come to know the fulness of both his love and our freedom.
Henri Nouwen

No church today can convince me that it is inspired until the words arising from it even in anger, break in a storm of beauty on the ear.
A.E

*I was angry with my friend,
I told my wrath, my wrath did end.
I was angry with my foe:
I told it not, my wrath did grow.*
William Blake

*Though thou with clouds of anger in disguise
Thy face; through that mask I know those eyes,
Which, though they turned away sometimes,
They never will despise.*
John Donne. (17th century)

ANGER

We've no doctrinal certainties about him or anyone else.
Nothing pinned to absolutes,
But thinking art and stories, thoughts scrabble among ruins.
Disorderly figure scrambling out of the background, he's picture-book as well as fiercest
Bible text, history's icon encrusted with duff clichés and religious labels.
Puff imaginative breaths and scrumptious narratives appear, the made-up more
glamorous than exactness, myths more interesting than facts, every
supposition beyond "the waggery of chance." 1.

BEYOND MEASUREMENTS OF KNOWING

Dark eyes emanating mischief, provocative and deliberate of speech, he's confusion
beyond summary, otherness loitering in the background, a pebble on a beach,
the same among many yet different.
Stepping near he recedes, always varying with the temperament of the viewer while
refusing to be a padded pillow, fired at and hit without making an impression.
Insidiously ambiguous, threatening yet fascinating, he arrives askew when he should be
vertical.
Expecting logical thinking, it's cryptic, anticipated in Jerusalem could find him in
Meccah, instead of centre he slinks into backgrounds.
Confounding comprehension, refusing diminishment to doctrinal clarity, scorning
formality and convention, he's a hall of mirrors, a knot to unpick, a secret to
sort out – hiddenness and unexpectedness slinking behind a person until taken
by surprise to find him there.
With clear understanding out of reach, I presume possibilities.

HOLY TYRANNY

No rigid figure adorning oil paintings or *"Gentle Jesus meek and mild,"* but slumbering
authority ready to awake, a gift of silent sympathy until aroused.
Enfant terrible, stirrer, dissident and *"shout in the streets,"* 2. less tame than he's made
out to be.
Courting outrage, never seeking adoration, he confronts.
A verbal alchemist, agitator and standing aggravation, his every word possessing
annoyance value.
With little demure, told to be quiet he shouts louder, a shrieking wind blowing where it
wishes, an arch trespasser following no patterns and obeying no recognised
law.
Dodging efforts to be worshipped, he's hard to have around, his presence disturbing, his
absence a relief and never dancing without treading on toes.

Puncturing pretensions, majestically disrespectful, an irritant throwing people off
 balance, shocking and confusing in his indifference, ever attracting while
 driving away.
No striving to be liked, efforts to be charming or flattering into well-being but directness,
 rigor and violence without pretension or vindictiveness.
In appetising danger and beautiful risks, he's jittery as a gunfighter, annoying as a wasp
 in a room, a fly buzzing in church.
Advocating revolt not submission, if he's not causing trouble, something's wrong.
Never shocked just disinterested, in cold suddenness alarming transformations.
Suffocated by fettered obedience, snarling beliefs, Sabbath laws, long prayers,
 nauseating fasts and subjugated womanhood, he turns like bottled milk
 abandoned in sunshine, anger always positive when correctly applied.

Artless and erratic among experts in spiritual fault-finding, weakest one becomes
 brawler, individuals leaving him cold one moment enrage in another, his anger
 momentary not prolonged.
Signals sent, cauldron lids raised, he stares, yelling with looks before opening mouth.
Void of tight-lipped meekness, capable of cursing, indignation becomes protection from
 power and hypocrisy.
Desiring disruption, disturbing equilibriums of respectability, less a rebel, more original,
 he rises from his naughty chair, kisses becoming bites in holy malice and
 impulsive innocence.
To remain interesting, one can't afford to be modest – if he was gentlest lullaby we'd
 doze off.
Accepting lunch from a Pharisee, the guest is churlish to his host – such audacity, but
 no one tells Seers how to behave!
Snapping, scowling, dangerous to talk to, toddler rage careers through crowded streets,
 every shout of anger an act of faith.
Little composure, but all you see you get, no compassion without indignation, vague and
 insipid without severity, puddles as well as ponds reflecting sunlight – even he
 wasn't 'good' all of the time!

FRONTIERS OF TENSION

From flowers bees invent both honey and venom, the *Seer* arriving to bless also comes
 to curse.
A wrecker crashing into legalism, watertight texts and list-making leaders.
If judgemental neighbours failed to squirm, his thinking was powerless.
Twitchy and cantankerous, he curses a fig tree, refuses to be tyrannised by rules,
 chases pigs over precipices, exorcises screeching spirits and like myself,
 irritable and out of patience when tired.
Prudent he couldn't be, opposites always complimenting one another.
"When he was good he was very, very good, but when he was bad he was horrid," 3. no
 one accusing him of being insufficiently human.

A pounding in fevered temples, unease and change in temperature, heated water producing steam, cold water creating ice – never anger without causes: a balance of tenderness and rage, his violent words cloaking fragile thoughts.
Conquering by obstinacy, anger double-edged, ratty, impatient, outspoken, even to his mother and shouting when he should be praying, companiable anarchist incites quarrels at religious retreats.

Dots aren't joining up.
What's happened to tact and civility?
Was he Jewishly obstinate and reverently opinionated?
When is obedience good and when not?
Never putting a foot wrong could be not putting it anywhere, so better breezy defiance than self-righteousness, hatred than bland indifference or simulated love in efforts to be esteemed.
Niceness infers dullness and anyone who can't get angry is less than human.
Tickle him, but momentarily he doesn't giggle, prick him, he refuses to bleed, raging words thundering, *"I don't like you,"* inner conviction cooing, *"But I care and forgive you."*
Do we hear swish of sword returning to its scabbard?
Love mingling with irritable sensitivity it's, *"I loath and detest you,"* in hasty words but inner music lilting, *"I'm caringly concerned about you."*
Tenderness beneath rudeness, the voice of obstinacy decides to give in.
Maybe greater the malicious attacks, more the good-humoured response, smilingly apologetically when hurt into retreating, building with similar actions with which he tears down, if so, we must overlook whimsy or incertitude.
Unlike some followers with insatiable appetites for punishment, perhaps more cartoon violence than real,
A timidity in mockery, a comic severity, his threats and ferocities applied with good humour.
Suffering fools gladly, terrible yet kind, sweet ridicule whips the kennel to teach the dog.
Never twisting the knife he prods with a stick, humour cauterising painful rebuke.
No one has a right to be feared.
Flippant and dismissive, maybe he felt sorry afterwards, requesting their names, inviting them to supper, mercy always annulling retribution, shabby carpets beaten not to destroy but remove debris.
Fragmenting dogma, rage is energised by goodwill.
Dismantling narrow-mindedness, he must be forgiven for being right.
Confused, rebellious, and poised to commit ghastly indiscretions, with uproar and shouting, slammed doors and scattered bedclothes, wrathful antics spit chaos onto busy streets.
Dragging clerics backwards and forwards, doctrinally pushing them around, sparring, insulting, stamping under foot and hating their orthodox smiles, he's a fly that needs swatting, a catalyst of emotions with grievous results, a brawler belching prophecy when everything spoken, happens.

ANGER MIXED WITH PLEASURE

Was he intimidated by his brashness?
Naughtily, like ourselves, maybe he secretly aspired for notoriety, or were there second thoughts and delayed regrets, meanings differing in colour and weight among different personalities?
Bark more than bite, purity of strength rather than humility with tears, he's reckless honesty and virtue in revolt, even provocation, gesticulating at enemies to raise conflicts, pleasure in disconcerting people, enjoying verbal scraps and shock effects, crowds always fascinated by rebels and street fighters.
Man of integrity, eyes alight with war, menace wrestles with emotion!
Edgy and irritable, disagreeable kindness pities the oppressed and rebukes the oppressor.
Affection for some, pulling faces at others, he desecrates flower beds in outlaw energy.
Warning sobriety and narrow-mindedness to keep their distance, he arrives to grasp not save, the true artist ready to disregard, deface and even destroy.
Violence playing like comedy, knotted rope between clenched fists, tables are kicked, chairs smashed, market stalls trashed.
Shaking a surly fist it's: *"Sod off from my Father's house!"*

Whatever did he do to relax?
Did he laugh at himself?
Was he bored sawing familiar wood, nailing same old planks and tolerating the cantankerous?
Like ourselves, moments of playful release, compensations for vocational pain and welcome escapisms, after all, it's tedious being holy all the time.

FLASHING EYES AND CURLING LIPS

Kill or cure, activist more than statesman, he invites storms, his dark side keeping him on edge, ferocity justifying jollity and mockery a weapon – anything but wishy-washy silence.
Swearing religiously sweetens his blood, sounds becoming clearer when tensions increase.
Stronger the light, sterner the shadow, the madder he gets more articulate he becomes.
Uncomfortable to be with, less consolation, more disturbance, notoriety propels him beyond an object of adoration, bandage of Sabbath devotion and guardian of propriety.
Upright among traditions, he opposes them, whisking rugs from under feet.
Angry man is cussedness you wouldn't dare tickle.
The last person to whom you would shout "Bo!"
Caressing like a mother, his anger becomes mercy yelling at kids too close to cliff-edges.

Is he man of fickle moods?
In afterthoughts, did he think himself silly?

While angry, is he angry with himself for being angry?
Erasing anger would destroy credibility – the grandeur of crags, agedness of oaks and
 elegance of antiquity.
Constrained like a kite he exerts himself, freed from revolt he'd hurtle to earth.
Shout him down, he'll raise a voice.
Compelled to conform, he's as dull as those he condemns.
Lawbreaker, agitator, wielder of humour and shadow.
Distractor, man of gimlet glance and arresting strangeness, he's humorous and grave
 without self-importance.
Principle apostle decreed: *"Obey those in authority over you."*
Sticking a tongue out, he bellows, *"Crap! I come to bring a sword,"* a weapon wielded for
 peaceful purposes."
If the flint is struck, expect sparks!
Refusing to sit on the fence because it hurts, weary of infantile attitudes, hair shirt
 dogma and *"for conscience sake"* statements not worth a strand of golden hair,
 Houdini wriggles out of rules, troublemaker yells "Fire!" in a theatre.
Ignoring boundaries, he must resist and won't let go.
At the end of his tether, he seethes at snobbery behind sacrosanct walls, doctrinal
 lunacies in dark corners and rampant hypocrisy driving him to do what he
 shouldn't.
Hating violated childhood, wildness reaches peaks of terrifying honesty and
 extraordinary savagery.
Buoyantly ogre-ish – Aspens shivering, Willows weeping, he hisses: *"Whoever abuses a
 little child let a great stone be hung around his neck so that he drowns in the
 sea."*

Virtue transcending fabricated prayers, he speaks in idioms, threats and comic severity
 badly interpreted by the partially enlightened mistaking ebb for flow.
When they understand his mercy, warnings become meaningless, anger of a kind
 person differing from anger of an evil one, and every threat of hell a divine
 deceit.
After all, it's fun frightening folk when there's nothing to be frightened of!
No decent person would inflict fiery punishment on another – God being a good
 Christian, or is he?
Smiling at terrors less vengeful more remedial, warnings never materialise, for why flee
 from wrath if its breath never brushes the cheek?
Recklessly exasperated, anger becomes a burden – not to crush but to carry.

RAGING AGAINST FANCY DRESS

"By his enemies you will know him."
No more bullies pushing religious terrors on burnt-out failures, but mocking pomposities
 and clever in put-downs, he wages comic assault on good taste.
Among harsh religious laws contrived by polite people, someone must resist.
Belittling moral achievements, the matador teases the bull: *"You pile burdens on
 people's shoulders never lifting finger-tips to help."*

Seeing drama in dullness, angry amazement evokes sarcastic answers: *"You practise piety so you can't be seen for who you are."*
To bluffers and pretenders, contemptuous dismissal: *"Hypocrites! You interpret the weather from the sky but can't interpret needs around you."*
Dripping sarcasm he scowls: *"You love best seats in the temple, congratulatory voices in town, but you're graves that people trample on."*
Tinily terrible, like children frightening pigeons: *"You criticise others yet never examine yourselves."*
Flippant at ceremonials he's a mick-taker: *"You religiously clean the outside of cups leaving the inside dirty."*
Guffawingly funny, religion is reduced to absurdity and amusement becomes instruction: *"It's easier for camels to scramble through a needle's eye than the greedy rich to enter eternal kingdoms."*
Humorously reducing life to absurdity, he jokes through clenched teeth: *"You strain insects from soup bowls yet gulp down camels."*
Wrong-footing his listeners, stealth humour shatters objections and added fun ridicules people who take everything seriously.
Laughing up his sleeve fearful of maligning the weak, some sniggered but only the wise understood.
Dissolving hypocrites to scorn, he crows: *"What good is it for one blind person to lead another if they both fall into a ditch?"*
"There's no scoundrels like respectable people," 4. and no one can be a hypocrite and not look it.
Wittily malicious he growls: *"They have their reward,"* or, *"Be careful what you want because you're likely to get it!"*
Imprisoning *God* in rigid rules, adherence to law undermining acts of mercy, he snarls: *"You serpents and vipers!"*
What a fabulist!
Politeness can be so bland and unconvincing.
Like sugar, fat and tobacco, he's a public health warning, cartoon terror becoming an art form and droll disgust nudging everyone to laugh at religion of the wrong kind.
Void of hate and vengeance, anger decrees that rage is morally permissible and spiritually productive, real violence occurring when it's kept inside and not let out.

FIGURE OF CHARM AND IMPULSE

Touch of the *scamp* agitates him!
A door slamming scampish-ness levelled at everyone's unpredictability.
With rustler's swagger he glares at traditions dented by overuse, an Artful Dodger outwitting enemies by playing into their hands, a beanstalk boy defeating giants by stealth and trickery.
Accused of heresy, the *Heretic* charges cynics with stupidity, none clever at being human.

But hearers can't hear – feet in the right place, ears upside down, they hurl loaded
    gestures: *"He's a friend of evil people. Possessed by Satan, that's why
    demons obey him."*

"This coin, is it Caesars?"
Look!
Fleas may be judging the dog but granny is devouring the wolf!
Bones tossed for chewing are spat out.
Cornered, he finds an exit, sensing intrigue a *storm departing* slips through back doors.
Another smile, he turns a corner and disappears, *"Chaoticist"* 5. refuses to be an insect
    in amber, confined to a library or esteemed in holy books.
Pastor warned, *"Don't let the sun set on your wrath,"* Seer responded, *"Red sky at
    morning (Good) Shepherd's **warning**!"*
Danger to religion and world, he won't be tamed and idolised.

1. Thomas Hardy.
2. James Joyce
3. Nursery rhyme.
4. Emile Zola.
5. John Cowper Powys.

SEXUALITY

Master Forstemius said that a certain brother named Lawrence, a Waldensian minister, had himself castrated in his youth and confessed that in his old age he regretted it for he burned with more desire than before. Dr Martin Luther replied: "Yes, indeed, eunuchs are more ardent than anybody else, for passion doesn't disappear but only power. For my part, I'd rather have two pairs (of testicles) added than one pair cut off.
Recorded in the Wittenburg Door. April/May. 1981

A council of Bishops held in Milan in 390 A.D excommunicated a monk. He wouldn't agree that "virginity is more meritorious than marriage.
Unknown

God himself dressed Eve's hair that the first woman might better please the first man.
Jewish Legend

We often find ourselves ... struggling against impulses and desires that we feel ashamed of, but in the end seem unable to resist. Our sense of shame is sometimes groundless, being merely the result of ideas about what is decent and proper that we have imbibed from our parents or the general atmosphere, though, if we really thought about it, we should realise that whatever we may be struggling against is as natural as eating and drinking, and indeed necessary for the development of our full personality. In such a situation, the worst thing we can do is to struggle against our desires in a negative sort of way. For by doing so we are concentrating our whole attention upon them, and so making them stronger rather than weaker: and if we succeed in suppressing them for the time being, we feel wretchedly frustrated until they rise to torment us once more. At the root of them lies the energy, the longing for fulfilment which is what makes us human beings, formed after the likeness of God.
Victor Gollancz

So closely are flesh and spirit intertangled in the web of our humanity that the flesh may actually feed and grow rampant upon the fervour of the spirit and, in the end, take terrible revenge.
H. Herma

Far better talk of nightingales, roses or women's eyes.
Ivan Turgenev

SEXUALITY

I'm thinking the unthinkable – pricking pins into the haphazard of
Christendom's hush-hush dilemma – his sexuality of which we know nothing.
Questions easier posed than answered and mysteries impossible to solve when I
    struggle to understand how Facebook works.
Approaching, odds and ends are snatched at, no exposition sufficing to reveal the man
    as he saw himself, a life not rigid but angular, perfection with flaws, a *"God*
    wanting to become man but not quite." 1.
Sensitive and complex, requiring re-definition in every age, he's becalmed by 'experts'
    who, like tourists not knowing the language, bellow louder to bewildered locals.
Christianity's dark secret and grand evasiveness is admitting he had sexuality,
    scriptures strangely silent, writers annoyingly mute.
Little knowledge may make us wise but I hope not!

BEYOND MEASUREMENTS OF KNOWING

Akin to ourselves, a synthesis of clashing impulses suffering storms of adolescence,
    teenage embarrassment, ambiguities of blushing puberty, shy desires and
    baffled lust.
Absence of child misbehaviour?
A flushed-faced Enid Blyton boy never telling fibs or having temper tantrums?
How horrifying, even in a chosen young man.
Urges can appear impure that in themselves are pure, as writer Paul perceived, *"virtue*
    perfected in the weakness of temptation," restless passions disturbing us more
    than Deity.
Our bodies not to be despised, everyone swapping innocence for experience in
    invasions of ardent longings, tussle of conscience, raging opposites, fury of
    awakened passions and inconvenience of concealing them; a magnificence
    disturbing and confusing in everyone drawing breath.
Never striving to be other than human, our ways of peeping at him could be wrong,
    short-sighted eyes out of focus, spectacles needing removal rather than putting
    on.
Kept under wraps, whitewashed from fleshly impulses in sermon and ritual, his sexuality
    is discussed by not talking about it in practised secrecy of religious
    disapproval; his happy mortality packaged into torrid saintliness and
    superhuman chastity.
Tragically diminished, he's become a pharmaceutical product, packaged, labelled, and
    tested harmless and beneficial.
Why was sexuality ignored by earliest apostolic writers?
Demeaned to chemist cleanliness, nudged into secrecy, his portrayed ambiguities build
    boundaries of ignorance and self-protection.
Embalmed in misconceptions, denying him wonders of embraces, nervous of losing
    their faith, threatened by cancelled salvation, fearful of heresy, blasphemy and

scared of damming penalties, fictitious images are furiously protected making Christians frightened of mercy as they are of judgment!

SENSUALITY AND SPIRITUALITY NEVER DISASSOCIATED

No divine short-circuiting but friendly wars between flesh and spirit, sensual and mystical unite in emotions not easily ignored.
For some, passions easily controlled, their morality lustreless, their stoicism dull.
In others, an inner spark easily fanned into consuming fires, spiritual and erotic dangerously allied for one to rouse the other and sudden passions not diminishing when occasions are removed.
Resembling us, the flesh frail and Eros ever seeking to assert itself, he wasn't protected by absence of desires or sudden impulses springing from attractions and affections – nothing being wrong with sex other than what's made of it.
Like regularity of winds and tides, flesh demands its rights, brain and body never exempt from emotional advances, the lion never tamed by locking it in a cage.
If so, his reputation could self-destruct in the thinking of his followers.
All life forms so orientated, *Grand Archetype* can't be excluded, natural instincts directing to creative roots of life, passion and desire physical symbols of yearnings after *Deity*.
To be unlike us, sexuality would be pointless, to be like us, everything coherent and rational, sexuality never separated from divinity.
Taking after *God*, translator of eager desires, denying him his birth-rights skirts on crime, suppressing his sexuality resorts to cruelty, contempt for the body an insult to creation.
For the blithe sex is sacred, at the heart an innocence.
To the spiritual nothing offensive, to the sensitive a moral compass, our fervours left to expand in sensitivity as well as fierceness.
Spirituality in erotic disguise, God not outside the body but unsoiled within it, *"purity being the power to contemplate defilement,"* 2. and romantic love reflecting deity embracing humanness.
If romance heightens spiritual feelings, how drab to be innocent not earthy, human but not sexual, living morally more than attractively.

THE QUICKENING EROS

Emotions in flux, for him, no hollyhock moments at feminine otherness, flashed smiles, and blushes of good-night glances?
Reaching beyond cool decorum, no females tweaking his sleeve, beckoning hands from behind closed curtains, swish of skirt and painted eyes prompting sentiments of *Song of Solomon* to dally in his thoughts: *"Your graceful legs are like jewels, your navel is a rounded goblet, your breasts are like two fawns, your eyes the pools of Heshbon."*
If holiness *"makes a man's face to shine,"* it also makes his hands sweat!
No intimate confidante, pretty temptations, saucy winks from women with mermaid blood and accidental nudges driving warm blood through throbbing veins?

Purer the life, more savage the desires when they come and, if a man reclined on his chest, why not a woman?
Or was he tormented moralist, *"a thing that was a man rather than a man?"* 3.
Body colliding with soul, did he yearn to clasp a woman in his arms, shrink from unhappy bachelordom, long for a family and father a daughter calling her Rachel?
But resisting marriage, no future dependents would fight over family connections.
In teasing momentum and admiration with or without touch, did controlled morality and uncontrolled emotions wage war?
Was concentration diverted by the tall and glamorous, glossy hair on promising shoulders, curve of thighs, pouting lips and swell of breasts – slinky tortures awakening worst and best.
If nothing makes the pure impure, wriggle-room must be made for the erotic, a dalliance with *"limb-loosening desire,"* 4. hormone-screaming confusion and heady suggestions not always understood.

VULNERABILITY VERSUS RIGIDITY

Surely irresistible urges sped through blood and brain, hating them worse than indulging them.
Plodding spiritual paths, was he never betrayed by gusts of temptation, moral strength and resistance never confined under Christian labels?
Was he innocently careless?
Were prayers abandoned for fun and feelings – springs of water both muddy and clear?
Yearning for something missing, did he come to terms with sexuality, those bottled-up passions stalking physical desire?
Without them, he's a sun circling earth, a planet lying flat, water flowing uphill, a rainbow emptied of colours – everything contradictory.
His dreams?
Sacred, sexual and others casting wonders on his world before frittering away.
Being a man of religious wrongdoing, he couldn't meet the people he did without glimpses of the soft and fascinating, teasing and beguiling.
Never terrorising into obedience, arousing fears or "Tut, tut" pretensions, no one is told what to do or how to behave.
Differing in thought, he never interfered with morality – smug intolerance enraging him not lowered standards, petty prohibitions not emotional neglect.
Uniting inconsistencies, he promotes more than constrains, never disapproving of human bodies, no imperfection regarded as disgusting.

MEEK INITIATES OR SOILED CHERUBS?

"Let us out of here! It's all a terrible mistake!" bark dreary saints and apostles hurling themselves through stained glass windows, their statements regarding God irritatingly inaccessible.
Are masks of propriety slipping?

Never disciples of restraint, they surely trifled with intimate miseries, if so, "boys will be boys," risking women's eyes and suggestive smiles to follow him more closely, their friskiness excusable in frolics of human passion.
Boisterous men of half-forgotten lusts and slippery sins, taunting, teasing and sniggering in *"pure-hearted wickedness,"* 5. ugliness in the painting not indicative of ugliness in the artist, cupidity and innocence needing to be lost in comedies of passion.
No paragons of modesty but boasters, braggarts of inoffensive vulgarity and harmless jollity daring each other in laddish humour and romantic vagaries.
Vices mixed with virtues, did they pray for strength to resist temptation while longing for opportunities of giving into it?
Sighs of relief at escaping danger, flickers of regret that it had not overtaken them.
Warming to discarded virtues, smashing rings of protective angels, enjoying bawdy jokes of Pharisee and belly dancer and like Luther, skittishly unafraid of vulgarity to humanise holiness.
Why not? The vulgar appear the happiest, their many improprieties mere simplicities.
What use is chastity without temptation – Simon Peter never reticent about cursing and swearing.
Curious but not indecent, godly words swallow coarseness rejected by the pious, crudeness of the crude majestic in the speech of the inspired.

Three years following him and no admiration of pretty smiles angering Dante and seducing De Vinci?
No burning blood and whispered gossip over flirtations at passing attractions, sinful smirks and hugs beneath haystacks, attractions into naughty complicities, rough oaths and frivolous patter over dramas of their love-lives or lack of it!
Winkingly suggestive, ruinous yet dazzling, no tantalising plums out of reach or rosy apples bruised when handled – titillated by encounters yet fearful of consequences?
Prayers in need of holidays, instincts conflicting with ideals and loss of self-control, sincerity of gospel writers aren't scandalised by their actions.
Less squandered morality, more naivete, failings never an impediment and God never needing rescue from voluptuous behaviour.
Not wishing friends to be saintly, absence of wit and masculine passions would make them uncontrollable, but in their company he's depth and elasticity – a conspiracy of banter and cheerfulness, their vulgarities evoking shrewd humour not pious rebuke –
Like ourselves, laughter brazen and flippant among many, but absent when alone.
Not prudish or a killjoy, dismissing their blushes, his frequent smiles are a challenge, the indelicate and scandalous never receiving saintly reactions from him.
From him no obscenities but playful beard strokes and arched eyebrows, wag of head at cocky overstated stories, friendly hand on the shoulder and when he winked at them, they grinned at him.
Never advocating fickleness or moral anarchy, devoutness roots itself in body as well as soul, his *God* seized with equal passion as man for woman.

MAN OF BROODING AWARENESS

He trilled that looking lustfully at women is equal to having sex with them.
The conjurer's sleight of hand trumpeting **statement** not warning, raspberry blowing not execution, for what man hasn't?
Don't be fooled!
Believers possessing gracious roguery as great as the convicted and imprisoned.
Never inflicting self-loathing on victims, he's sympathy for the seduced, playful warnings being, *"Why love chocolates to abandonment when they make you sick?"* chocolate the servant not the dictator.
With reckless gaze and grinding voice, he spits at feigned superiority: *"Look at your own life not other people's,"* men pooh-poohed as men, none treading in vertical directions, no restraints without passions, all suckers for self-interest, only quitting power after falling from it.

If the woman was *"caught in the very act,"* flickers of sexuality were glimpsed by him as well as others.
Jumping on sins because custom tells them, enemies stretch their claws, but grabbing their soiled laundry he hurls it skyward for all to see.
Void of rule-book morality, strong in principle, gentle in blame and supreme in cunning, barbed hooks are hidden inside lollipops of stupendous mercy.
Unlike church gifting in forbidding and restricting, advising and interfering; less bothered about "sins of the flesh," he rages against 'sins of the mind,' sex ever the goblin mask of seven deadly ones.
Applauding instead of condemning, peeping beyond appearances, he's aware that beatific decorum isn't detached from sexual attraction.
Sincerity concerns him, not 'sinfulness.'
With little to forgive, he forgives little, most people not wanting evil but falling into it, scruples raising them above physicality, spirituality of the wrong kind dragging them down.
In dainty triumph, the fly is released before the spider pounces.
No prudish embarrassment or tainting with shame but empathy and shameless glee.
Vice bores him – other issues are more important.
When he's about, wickedness isn't easy!

TANTALISED BY EMOTIONAL SUGGESTIONS?

At awkward moments in a watching house, his feet are drenched in twilight hair and strangling fragrances.
Symbols of honour, insinuating, larky, provocative?
Are feelings juxtaposed with fancy and confusion? *"Her many sins are forgiven; for she loved much."*
How torturous wanting things you can't have.
Maybe innocent dalliance never reached beyond faltering glances, his visionary objectives controlling wayward impulses without cramping them.
Or was he out of place like birds of paradise in neighbourhoods of sparrows?

Did masculine blood shriek into fire with only fire to answer it?
If so, he equalises with us instead of condemning us.

And Magdalene Mary?
No shared walks beside silvered seas and a pale lover's moon?
Did desire grab him amid goat bells tinkling in fading light, dizzy scent of orange
> blossom, that bracelet of amber, those flashing eyes beneath drooping lids – a
> delicate precariousness when *Omnipotent God* could eagerly become man?
Were there flashing signals and responses read into?
Passion innocent among crowds, impish when there's one person and that one a
> woman!
Not forgetting the nameless lady at the water well.
Perceiving muddled emotions and many marriages, he twitters, *"Would you give me a
> drink?"*
Teasing reproof in play it's, *"Why not go home and call your husband?"*
Second-sight or glimmers of cupidity at first glance?
Kittenish, eyes dark as damsons crammed with secrets, the coquettish drop of a
> handkerchief for him to pick-up?
Shared uncertainty beckoning beyond borders?
Threatened and vulnerable – a gigantic boulder finely balanced, ready to totter at brush
> of fingertips, or is he strong enough to peep over precipices without losing
> balance, his modesty fictitiously his greatest attraction.
After all, he's no inventor of Bible texts, trafficker in guilt or fanatic in holiness.
Embarrassingly unaware, perhaps he wasn't aroused, underlying emotions fast asleep.
Trivialities no more urgent than wasps storming windows, tenderness requiring no
> intimacy, passions stifled but never far away.
The vigour of non-sexual love as intense as genitally operated love, attractive to men
> and women without being attracted to them, or he responded in normal ways
> as it seemed in an old-world garden.

Mary, bosom deep in sunflowers catches a cautious voice, *"Don't touch me!"*
> *"Don't come too close!"* or *"Cease clinging to me!"*
Needing depth and intensity, comfort and reassurance, she yearns to connect and
> belong.
"You are more intimate to me than I am to myself," sighed Augustine, aware that God's
> "touch" is more than a figure of speech.
We touch things we care for, our hands the flexibility of our thoughts. *"If I can but **touch**
> his hem,"* simmered a sickly lady, the sweet aroma of touch being the
> heartbeat of the senses – no touch, no sensitivity.
Touching, insisted Aristotle, the *"basis of all senses,"* a prized gift of humanness making
> his every touch a surprise.
Sensitivity in fingertips, gentle curiosity strokes a child's cheek and gently squeezes a
> follower's arm.
But this moment, butterfly vulnerability flutters in cavernous eyes, timidly needing
> affection but hesitant when it's offered.
Refusing garden clinch, he won't let go.

Passing gusts of temptation?
Delicate shyness? Ambivalent desire?
Passions gaining strength, knowledge of humanness blushingly beautiful in gentle smiles of, *"I can't,"* limits seen not as walls but skylights.
No suppression of attractions but pretending not to hear.
A looking over the shoulder and ignoring, "nudge, nudge, wink, wink" never denying sex but ignoring it – not all risks being his risks.
Aware that immoveable convictions kill quests for truth, I grope among questions with wagtail hesitation.
But why are the 'godly' hard on themselves and others?
Why gorge guilt, flagellate with regrets and let-rip condemnation?
Reckless passions raging within, we could try being soft, giving *him,* ourselves and others affectionate coffee-breaks.
Surpassing understanding, passions offer direction as we travel toward wholeness *not* perfection – nothing added but much enjoyed in daring adventures of human existence.

1. C.G.Jung
2. Simone Weil.
3. Charles Williams.
4. Sappho.
5. Iris Murdoch.

MADNESS

The time is coming when people will go mad, and when they meet someone who is not mad, they will turn to him and say, "You are out of your mind," just because he is not like them.
Abbot Anthony. Desert Father

The more a soul conforms to the sanity of others, the more does it become insane.
Mary Webb

O king of glory, who needs no drums and banners, you have made me mad, and madmen live beyond law. Therefore be bewildered and distraught, nothing less, so that God's help may come to you from before and behind. Abandon security and stay in frightful places! Throw away reputation, become disgraced and shameless! I have tested the far-seeing intellect – after this I will make myself mad. Sell your intellect and buy only bewilderment! Such a purchase will bring you gain.
Rumi

When the influence of grace becomes strong, it is surprising how exhausting it is to the spirit, even though it causes pleasure. And it is very exhausting to the body too, if it is felt often. When this influence of grace comes on strongly, it throws the body into convulsions suggestive of madness or drunkenness.
The Scale of Perfection. 1494

*Ragged and queer and old, he comes alone,
But sometimes with mysterious smile,
He mutters to himself the while,
Or stops to hold strange converse with a stone.
Ah, men beware lest you should curse
The Master of the Universe.*
Celia Duffin

*The madman is not the man who has lost his reason. The madman
Is the man who has lost everything except his reason*
G. K. Chesterton

MADNESS

Beyond analyses, profuse in disguises and sculptured into hyperbole,
He's shards of glass shaken into unexpected designs.
A plodding anachronism and wandering intensity with thoughtful eyes, too vast for one book and one church, double meanings and legitimate exaggerations making him master of hints more than seller of certitudes.
Emotional more than cerebral, rugged, broody, leading people astray, he hurls himself into humanness.
An upside-down reflection in a pool, a man of metaphysical extravagance, consuming vision, brooding enthusiasm and consecrated eccentricity.
Like Blake, Boehme, Theresa and other mystics wielding worrying symptoms of disordered lives, he inhabits universes where few intrude, speakers of penetrating things always misunderstood by the masses.

SEEING WHAT WE HAVEN'T RECOGNISED

Crazed by sweetest emotions, gluttonous for existence, *"In him was **life**,"* surf and wave plunging and heaving, his reckless zeal sacrificing dignity to ideal ends.
Leaping extravagantly into life, prepared to become disagreeable and dangerous, he scatters drama and effect.
With no rules but his own fervour, mad mortality expands in huge awakenings, boisterous intensity teetering on lunacy yet never hostile to reason.
Stupors pitching him by the road, madness carefully calculated, eccentricities cartwheel into ridiculousness and inner meanings exhaust themselves in unsettling appearances.
Knowing his own mind or does he, the dividing line between poet and oddity tissue thin?
Hiding our own peculiarities as well as his, a strangeness in us all, everyone suffering torments of madness.
Everyone damaged, neurotic and fallible in one way or another while remaining perfectly sane.
Alive in significance, person of dark charm and independent thought, beyond truth or error, profundities dip into peculiarities.
Vastness clinging to smallness, exalted moods dash into ridicule making him opposite persons at the same time.
Dismissing tired religion, thinking on crooked lines, misfit thunders into life, an intoxicated bee in a flower, every quirkiness void of discretion.

SPECIALIST IN THE OUTRAGEOUS

Illogical? That's his way of existing, an innocence residing in insanity.
Only the stirred-up inspire, fresh creative thoughts always sounding mad.
Eccentric and original, some must be believed because they are so absurd.

Exaggerating, he must strike human imagination with divine absurdities, his enthusiasm
    evoking heavenly tricks better doubted than analysed.
With taints of the bizarre, in creative brilliance he rides untamed mules,
    hurls curses at a fig tree,
    bellows rebukes at raging gales,
    raises the dead back to life,
    freewheels heresy,
    spits into a person's eye,
    chats with screeching demons,
    conjures a coin from a fish's mouth,
    mass produces sandwiches to feed multitudes,
    promenades across water and other spoofs exquisitely Quixotic and scattily
        never done before, every 'miracle' prompting belief not because of
        but in spite of.
Epitomising a *Wild* God, too much of the unusual can be disquieting, but if
    performances aren't accepted for all they are, we must welcome everything
    possible.
Genius married to madness, no artist, poet or prophet authentic unless they break rules.
Brimming with surprises, crammed with contradictions, *"the moth of madness throws
    itself at the candle of love."* 1.
Like wrack thrown-up by the sea, inspected and tossed back, he's mysterious to himself
    as well as others, out of step now as he was then.
Why not? It's rarely the imaginative who turn crazy.
In art we go abstract, in music avant-garde, both arousing feelings more than
    knowledge.
Better exalted hallucinations and doctrinal foolery than boredom, routine and repetition,
    making madness more beguiling than sanity.

MADNESS SALTED WITH WONDER

"Who does he think he is?"
"He's demon-possessed and raving mad. Why listen to him?"
He's mad because he differs from others, from now on words and actions will be
    labelled lunacy.
Society wants to cure him, but the only way to cure is to kill!
If he's mad, the religiously sensible are the cause, thus cancelling it out.
The eccentric being the most interesting, their 'madness' never hiding God.
Deaf and blind to public opinion, emotional more than mechanical, gusto arouses
    recklessness, his kindness and compassion like strong wine overturning sense
    and reason.
Brain cogs disturbed, the wise and loving are easily 'mad,' everyone needing an
    illuminating religion of wildness, not counting leaves on trees, cracks in
    pavements, mumbling at the moon and other goofy stunts, but controlled
    madness of one who's fathomed the orthodoxy of which they've rebelled.
Withdrawn from law and religion his head swims with vision, only the disturbed plumbing
    depths of innumerable emotions.

No paranoia, more spiritual rapture beyond certification, sanctity crouched in anomaly, innocence in eccentricity, symptoms earning little discredit in his day while raising echoes in our own.

Semitic in temperament, riotous in blood-type, distracted by contradictions and bereft of dignity, madness is his fight to exist:
Vertigos of wisdom rocketing beyond level-headed logic into noisy mutterings of *"an extraordinary being mad in one century as another."* 2.
Feeling God as aches and agony, he suffers Judean effusions of the euphoric, doses of ecstasy, intoxication without wine and dizzy spasms celebrating *God* the *Grand Enchanter* – a bird released from its cage in antic disruptions of restless joints.
Spiritual combustions of jumping, hopping and clapping hands – body actions personally human, alive to feelings of being himself and mad in sanest, sensible ways.
Seismic beliefs lived out with life and limbs, hands, arms, knees and legs in dancing contortions.
In a despondent world of inflexible rule and law, extremes were necessary so that mercy and freedom could explode into life.
He's out of himself in passion for *God* and people, performing messages as well as speaking them.
Accept him as eccentric, but don't lock him away as lunatic.
To know God intimately he would stand on his head or hop all day on one leg, but it's risky worshipping *deity* emotionally, freedom to be demonstrative being pleasure as well as curse, but how delightful being one's-self!
Instead of falling apart, like clowns and actors he's tragi-comedy, tongue and lips not the only gifting of story tellers.
Interpreting *God* eccentrically without loss of integrity, there's irony in his gestures.
Arousing the spectacular, majestic madness in wisdom of the mystics possesses him.
Experiencing divine vibrations, he responds to music from other worlds, if needs be, like King David, stripping off clothes to dance naked before *deity* – few devotees ever swallowing such irregularities.
Is he making a fool of himself?
Ah! It's the mad who pay the redemptive price for those of us who prize our sanity!
If he's neurotic, fault lies with immoveable religion; moved to broadminded atmospheres, he's poet, heretic and orator.
Depth and stillness will return, but momentary, a *"limb-loosing love"* 3. for God, passion and fury signs of inner stability, fiercest joy saving him from madness not driving him to it.
If *Deity* condones fundamentalist theatricals of media evangelists eager for camera angle in stunning suits and lacquered hair, why be gloomy over spiritual lunacies?
Everyone's religious experiences involve some degree of mental agitation.

IGNORING THE MADMAN

"Stop him someone!"

But excess has become moderation, his madness ringing with importance.
Life can't be solemnised unless lived impetuously and chaotically, flirting with darkness, waltzing in light, disbelief as well as faith – otherwise, no knowing!
A learning over and again the gift of existence, every new day chaos and mystery in contrast to strict arrivals, tidy luggage and dated ticket.
Dazed by insight, his spirituality un-expressed without hysteria, he must cherish his mania.
Careless in ecstasy, spirit escapes body as sunshine sucks moisture.
Emotions un-maintained, *God Unnameable* sings inside him.
Soaring like a lark, plummeting like a gannet, he spends himself beneath mad skies and drunken moons – greatest moments ending in gloom, every enlightenment transitory, but when delirium subsides his message remains and idiocy redeems.

"And when his family heard (him), they went out to take charge of him, for they said: **'He's out of his mind,'** *he's mad!"*
Perhaps the kindest way of looking at things, but where's the wisdom isolating holy madness behind locked doors?
The same be said of every luminary feeling, strange exhilaration and restless aspiration.
There's a wonder about hysteria!
In matters of changing truths, one must be eccentric, divisive and heretical.
Worse than locking him out, they scheme to lock him in!
But he's too inimitable to be caged and confined, imprisonment would make him madman in an attic.
Suffering torments of madness, he's perfectly sane.
   "Call a doctor, find an exorcist!"
   "He must pull himself together!"
   "What will the neighbours think?"
   "Subdue him with sedatives, keep him from danger!"
   "He's talking strange things we can't grasp."
Every hoot and cackle the hostility of the normal toward the abnormal.
Nobody knows what to do!
Does no one understand that he's a joke as well as a threat?
"Let him who is without neurosis cast the first stone." 4.
Digging in heels, 'odd man out,' he embarrasses his family, mystifies friends, annoys neighbours and becomes gossip of the town.
"His enemies shall be those of his own household."

DIZZY AND DISORIENTATING

Aware of his madness he can't be demented, fiery emotions – his and ours, allied to psychosis, many having imagined visions, guiding voices, hysteria and other ecstatic over-reactions making it risky being dissident when everyone's regimented!
Dancing the world to pieces, he's not normal, sense and fancy overlapping genius where boundaries lack certainties: *"Keep him indoors!" "Lock him up!"*

Awakening sleep, he lobs incredulity on everything concealed, madness that isn't mad restraining madness that is.
Amid theological muddles, crowds demand doctrinal definitions, but none are possible.
Vision giving space for the frenzied, his wildest revelations stated but not explained.
"If you would know who I was: in a word, I am the Word who did play at all things and was not ashamed. **Twas I who leapt and danced**,*"* sang the gnostic Hymn of Jesus.

Chasing the unexpected, imprisoned impulses break out to devour him.
Slippery, he can't be pinned down.
In ecstasy and despair he totters on edges of darkness, high tensions and wild fatigue propelling nervous systems to breaking point, directing toward a nursing home, confining to an asylum, rescuing from the moon.
Swerving from the norm he's crazy, but what is normality?
Maybe little more than cultural make-believe, everyone a collision of freakish contradictions making square pegs and round holes obsolete.
If enthusiasm is proportional to sanctity, then the mad have more insight than the sane.
When believers rate rare in understanding, richest revelations leap from eccentric outsiders.
If all disorder is divine order misunderstood, then he overstrains genius, blinking at visions, shattering conceptions and overturning understanding.
Comfortable with his peculiarity and knowing his demons, he plays with them.
Healing his madness would eliminate his virtues.
Daydreams to one, reality to another, by remaining odd he becomes an exception – *"the stone which the builder rejected,"* stones de-railing trains, paving blocks tripping runners.
Certain in the thrill of the chase, high tensions produce big sparks, clear and muddled opinions overlap, but from dreams, seizures and hallucinations, meanings gather.

IN TOUCH WITH THE ETERNAL

Awash with would-be saviours, mountebanks and wandering wizards, raging prophets were common sights, screaming spells and incantations, imbibing music to stimulate visions and matching the mad in fury.
In eccentricity he stays sane – musical discord intervened by other notes resolving themselves into rarest harmonies.
Bellowed threats never halt wild waters.
There's method in his madness.
One with glowing eyes won't be cribbed and crabbed.
Bending no rules except his enthusiasms, it becomes *"a great temptation to go mad,"* 5. religion attracting far-seeing half-wits and society needing absurdity like burnt earth needs rain.
Cranks, oddities and mavericks braving psychic storms and skewered insults.
Oddities with human faces joining hearers of voices and thinkers of strange things.

Is their state worse than ours, requesting logical explanation and literal translation of impossible mysteries?
Impulsive as a child, volatile as chemicals, he suffers maddest consequences of artist and poet, revolutionary and romantic, beating heart and thudding nerves evoking swings from pain to pleasure.
Not unhinged dementia or religious frenzy but respectful **"Hypomania."**
> "Filled with energy, flooded with ideas, restless and unable to keep still, channels energy into achievements of wildly grand ambitions; little sleep, feels brilliant, especially chosen, perhaps even to change the world; a risk taker, charismatic and persuasive, prone to making enemies…" 6. attributes of anyone prey to joyful insanities.

MANIACAL SENSE OF ORDER

Out of his mind? Neurotic?
Revelation tripping from edginess, his madness is society's sanity, the tap appearing dirty but the water clean.
"If we are **mad** it is for God; if we are rational, it is for each other, for the love of Christ constrains us."
Glimpsing the unseen, the mad become mad having escaped from adult games, disembowelled wonder and religious role play.
Pricking bubbles of power and performance, leaping up and down on dogma and order, the 'mad' Jesus shrieks that beliefs become too dogmatic, too hygienic, respectable, self-satisfying and obsessive.
When mad thoughts possess the sincere, *none* can be *sincerely* wrong.
Madness in him, folly in us?
At home with his madness, perhaps he's pretending to be sane!

1. *Rumi.*
2. *G. K. Chesterton.*
3. *Sappho.*
4. *Iris Murdoch.*
5. *George Elliot.*
6. *John Gartner.*

DOUBT

Recently, I read with wry amusement a news item about a priest who volunteered to take a lie-detector test on television. During the interrogation he was asked, "Do you believe in God?" He answered, "I do." The detector recorded his answer as a lie! I chuckled at his embarrassment, but I pitied him too. Life itself is the best of all lie-detectors. All of us carry around with us a baggage of unexamined credos and untested convictions. All of us discover sooner or later, what cobwebs we have clung to in the dark.
Morris West. A View from the Ridge

He believes and disbelieves with impassioned confidence, I want to see him doubting.
S. T. Coleridge (a letter to a friend)

Those who believe that they believe in God but without any passion in their heart, without anguish of mind, without uncertainty, without doubt, without an element of despair even in their consolation, believe only in the God-idea, not in God Himself.
Miguel de Unamuno

Imagine a man in hiding and he stirs, he shows his whereabouts thereby; and God does the same. No one could ever have found God; he gave himself away.
Meister Eckhart

*An angry old Anglican swore
He'd lost his faith so he tore
His Bible to pieces,
Burned pictures of Jesus,
But God loved him still, maybe more.*
Garrison Keillor

*All the more a spirit gay, breathes within my heart a rhyme,
'Tis but hide and seek we play in and out the courts of time.*
A.E

DOUBT

Living where we live, London, Dublin, New York or wherever,
Would make him silence-greedy now as then.
Ponderous disappointments pursue impressive careers and after huge stress, emptiness!
Under threat and demand, poisonous hurry and furious discouragement, he's no exception.
Battered and bewildered he needs to meander, too many voices in one room, jangling crowds shunting him from one corner to another.
Cheering-up isn't the answer, he must sneak away from public places and senseless chatter, his inside child screaming for silence, his inner disquiet begging re-orientation.
Windows need opening, pauses snatched that straying light may finger his soul, gripped stillness leading to rest and pin-drop silences creeping from afar.
Prattling Aspen trees hold their breath, floating thistle seeds flower when motionless, rivers reflect clouds when calm, dew gathers in silence, but this moment a trapped fly buzzes behind blank glass.

Doing nothing is difficult to do, but things aren't made to be busy, merely allowed to happen.
In non-doing, occurrences occur – they've always been there, he hasn't.
He must become idle and light-hearted so that his soul can grow.
Life sits down when he sits down, a sagging spirit needing to flop and sprawl – even *God* working so slowly needed rest!
Bruising demands must cease, then he'll become a stroller – delaying inspiration instead of dashing into it.

WHISPERS IN THE MOUNTAIN

Hankering after the inconspicuous, attracted by far-offs, *"He withdrew himself into the mountains alone,"* arc of earth rising to greet him.
Mountains make one feel small – he desires smallness, the smaller we feel, more dependent we become.
Craving repose he escapes haste, a slowing down, a freedom from suddenness.
Strange pressures of *Image Maker* are crashing upon him.
On journeys of discovery, doubts, uncertainty and temptations are inevitable.
Constant loving can be wearing, *God's* intrusions elaborate and demanding, everyone needing rest from religious compulsion, no one surviving ardours of spiritual gratification.
Convalescence from divine demands is needed, holy things aren't making sense.
But maybe spirituality isn't meant to be sensible.
Didn't he argue with religious believers, his disciples disagreeing, his followers tetchy, quarrelsome and intense?

Perhaps division is disguised near-ness not far-ness – stinging bees and fragrant flowers needing each other.
Shouting echoes of frustration and hearing them fade away, from rowdy streets to hidden caves, outsider stalks dizzy ledges, speaking precipices and wild gorges splintered into silence.
Among noble serenity and hideous romanticism, higher he climbs the more restless he becomes.
Clawing in canyons still as statues, edging round precipices on hands and knees, listless eyes lift to glimmering moonlight and crags etched into sunsets.
Warmed by leaping flames at night, wall shadows remind and depress.

Suffocated by misunderstanding, used and dropped like sweet wrappings, destiny needs coordinating.
Treading life's stage is one thing, stepping out at the right moment another.
Others can't be inspired if he's flagging himself.
Dithering, he must return to leaden days, disturbed nights and deep crowds, candles have been burning both ends, jangled nerves wincing under lashing looks and verbal blows.
Is he fading before he's made his mark?
Living on his nerves, he aches for solitude and a life of his own.
To walk inside himself meeting no one.
No nagging crowds, pleading hands greedy for miracles and pressure to "spread a message" – just space to breathe and restore harmony.
He once barked, *"Come to me weary people and I will give you rest."*
Now he must practice what he preached!

Twitchingly alone, there's freedom to shout, scream and kick his world to pieces.
Walking with no one watching – looking, listening, feeling, like a sombre owl with only the moon to speak to, he needs restfulness without interruption, requesting nothing from anybody nor they from him.
Sitting silent an obvious, swinging aside from clucking admiration, he must *"learn the miracle of restraint,"* 1.
Too much is being done – his soul needs a holiday.
Burnout bordering breakdown, wounded and depressed, heightened emotions battle frustrated hopes – the dying fish most active when removed from its environment, a building on fire burning brightest before collapsing.
In life's menagerie, sensitive natures attract deepest despondency, zeal vanishing when pursued, best objectives never equalling highest expectations, given measures of peace unsustainable.
Commitment is arduous when fatigue erodes but *"Blessed are those who aren't happy with who they are."*
Travel must be gentle, not vehement.
No miracle mongering, no submission to audience demands.
"Talkative little Christianity." 2. is stifling internal whispers, the more zealous religion becomes, more ferocious the thirst of its followers.

Strength is needed to be still, wisdom to hasten slowly, carried along by non-action,
   drifting instead of navigating, floating with the current and going where the
   slope leads.
Exiting the cavern, he heads for the seashore.

SONG OF THE SEA

"That same day, Jesus went out ... and sat by the lake."
Lured by journeying sunlight, quiet niches hollowed out of hubbub are sought.
Like beckoning drugs, he sneaks toward seashore solace among tufts of sea-thrift,
   stones smelling of sunlight and thin scream of seabirds in empty skies.
People behave differently at sea- sides, galloping waves and kissing foam calming
   anxieties, relaxed and uninhibited, they become gods, dreamers and
   romantics.
Blinking in sunlight, weary of sitting, clothes are hurled aside – naked man in winking
   water, a tired body in unruffled pleasure.
Sweat and stress slide away – silvered seas feel for him, every ripple an emotional
   connection.
Happily deprived of conversation, reposing in immediacy, he ceases to be puzzled by
   callings and objectives.
A spent mind mends itself, everything easing back together.
Beneath shimmering reflections, cloudless worlds engulf and cure.
Sinking, rising, swigs of air are snatched before submerging.
He's fathoming depths of offered peace, a bubble of solitariness dropping into reticence,
   the muteness of Joseph listening to Mary, a trance of *"emotions recollected in
   tranquillity,"* 3. weariness dipping into repose among softly streaking fish,
   faraway boats, dipping oars and lapis seas meeting lapis skies.
He floats in quiet thoughtfulness – a lily in an undisturbed pool, a return to child-ness,
   anxieties fading like stones dropped down deep wells.
Independent of everyone, seeing things from afar, questions creep dangerously through
   his mind:
   "*Why this rushing around?*"
   "*Is urgency an ingredient of God's plan?*"
   "*Is active devotion a smokescreen for 'be still and know,' and total commitment
   worth paralysing burnout?*"
Uncertain of truths requiring declaration, maybe it's best not to follow them, his
   meaningful uncertainties never drowned in indifference or aroused to loud
   disturbance.

Time hovers unmeasured in spread of brooding quietness, wash and undertow of
   feelings, delicious idleness and stumble of small waves defying everything
   except the moon.
Lessons hold breath, questions fade from thought; he drifts among nuzzling truths and
   fondling peace.
In idling immediacy, little need be done, no explanations, no one to meet, nothing to
   pursue,

God Ineffable the artist, he the model, motionless as water under ice, quiet as the breath of a sleeping child, serene as leafy branches on summer evenings.
Stillness fuses with becalmed immensity.
Wandering undertones invite him to listen, as in reading stories absent authors speak.
Sultry and adrift, eyes are shut in efforts to see, lips sealed from dirge of useless words for when wasted words cease to exist, real words abound.
Like the mirrored sea, he's distance and depth, fickle mood and isolation.
A jobless passer-by rising and falling in repose, a recluse in good-natured laziness.
Emptied of doing and moving, unlike followers crowing rights to speak and belligerent beliefs to defend, he hears all he needs to experience, not what he ought to learn.
An inner agreement, a given appetite to know and become – perhaps he knows already but can't recall or won't admit, knowledge residing in thoughts through language, or stealing noiselessly across the unuttered for *"He who knows God is dumb."* 4.
Abandoned and alone, sudden gusts annoy seaside silences, time loiters, nothing is urgent.
He's enjoying *Keeper of Secrets* whose sacred words reside in everyone waiting to be born.
But every mood demands an opposite and each feeling too good to last.
Like rising suns, sprightliness returns, frayed feelings spring to life.
Afternoon comes late, the sun drops over the edge of day.
Like the ocean, gently agitated, he paddles ashore, dresses and scrambles out of sight.

DESERT DESPAIR

Clocks strikes thirteen.
Ponderous toll of bells are carried on solemn winds. *"He left the Jordan river and was driven out into the barren desert where Satan tempted him forty days."*
Away from jabbered prayers, jostled into *God's* violence, in dumb dismay he's thrust into deserts brooding and waiting, a confused visitor in unfamiliar rooms.
Driven to torment beyond explanation, a period of groping – *Creator's* experiment in self-discovery, an oasis of perseverance among wilderness absurdity, less adventure, more ordeal.
Deserts are where battles are won or lost, so why choose this punishing path?
If I could have welcomed him into Sussex woods, he'd be happier knee-deep in bluebells, witchery of primroses, cloistered oaks and quiet ponds where herons poise on one leg.

Deserts are better imagined than experienced.
Crammed with nothingness, no one calls his name, no one's around to spend friendship on him.
Solitary souls face everything, painful aloneness growing like youth limping into adolescence, despairing silences like numbing news of a beloved's death.
But the stage being set, the drama must begin.

Pitting himself against the untamed, nomad staggers mute and alone, a lost butterfly in an empty room, a dragonfly reticent to settle.
Isolated, the plant struggles in under nourished soil, *Imminence* directing willing walkers and kicking those who drag their feet.
Senses sharpened by strangest sights and sounds, bullied by sunshine, menaced by evenings terrible with stars, he's footloose wanderer born-away like migratory birds, heartbeat and footsteps bleeding into backgrounds of dead stones and grasping thorn bushes.
Deserts deepen with infinitude of sand, howl of roaming animals and his own whinnying panic.
Threatened by desert quarantine, he's entered primal disorders of terrified breathing and nervous whispers, crude majesty casting contempt on maps and senses.
Faltering springs loiter long enough to dry up, rocks hotter than wagging flames, swirling dust of ruins come and gone, humming sand and stones silvered by moonlight.
Deserts, less absence of sounds more silence of doubts.
Abandoned, one is raped of will and resolution, a threatening otherness of sneaking presences and beckoning phantoms, robbers, wild beasts and mad hermits among absence of order where worst things happen unseen.
Beneath brassy skies, lizards pose motionless, scorpions creep into unsuspecting shoes and immense birds crank across blood-red skies.

Wastelands show little patience with holy thought, innocence provoking strangling desires and attempted seductions, dark moods and repeated hallucinations like night voices in upstairs rooms, creak of floorboards, dreams of horrors under beds and mutterings in ancient forests at dusk.
He frets, he falters – every encounter inflating panic and fear, no wonderment or aplomb but stripping of certainties.
No one to confide in, he's wrapped in threatening doubts and unutterable bewilderment – no sound, voice or vision.
"Why do I need to be here?"
"What purpose does it solve?"
"Have I lost my way and got it all wrong?"
Deity better understood through reckless disagreement than lame-dog submission.
Apprehensive and hungry, maybe he thinks of returning home.
Slumping wearily into shadows, he craves sleep.

THE DARK JESTER

Sunshine gobbles the day.
In deceit of sunset amid beating of wings, semblance of man stalks darkening horizons.
Charming yet illusive, impressive as biblical texts, arrogantly beautiful yet ingratiating,
Dark Invented One – a running figure lit by twitch of lightning.
No bony fingers, serpent eyes, vaporous threats and cantering hoofs, but bad blood in romantic grandeur trailing odours of spices.
Attractive as Nightshade, sticky with sentimentality and clutching beliefs as people carry diseases,

A *Voice in the Desert* snipes and wheedles, every breath bitter as cheap wine:
> "Is this man really so extraordinary?"
> "Who in hell does he think he is!"
> "Come on, throw your weight about," and other silly statements thought up by fools.

In respectful mockery, fairy godmother arrives for the christening speaking softly to those who catch its eye:
> "Master of Miracles. Why not stride forward and rule?"
> "Stand on temple spire. View your world and mine."
> "Enhance your reputation and save the suffering!"
> "Perform tricks. Change rocks to bread and feed the poor."
> "Grab kingdoms and form a personality cult."

Voices inside his head?
Days and nights without food?
Breathless and thirsty after stifling heat?
Like milk purring into pails, tricksy offers of unrequested influence, falsity sounding true, good sculptured into fraud, deceit cartooned as virtue, not doing wrong things but right things for wrong reasons, worst lies being closest to truth.

ISOLATIONS OF DOUBT

Path-finder totters undisturbed, or does he?
"The devil," as someone smirked, *"attacking whatever's hovering in the mind."*
Teetering between flattery and exhaustion, enticed from noblest aspirations to tricks of self-promotion, he could wield power without wisdom, side-stepping to starry moralist and applauding multitudes.
Or, like us, wooed toward divine things then shooed away, shaken by beliefs that lose their sting and ideals never quite attained.
Even the restrained question long-held values, reverting to paths first disapproved of and jilting convictions when they become an interference – no one certain of persevering to the end, everyone falling short of highest intentions, holiest feelings transitory, vehemence never sustainable and over-much zeal self-destructive.
Breath of *Highest One* suddenly awakens him!
Life, not passion to possess but desire to discover, no cosy victory but pensive and brooding,
Path-finder fears for himself and every believer, expert and leader aspiring influence and recognition, competition blowing through bloodstreams, glow of supremacy in every garland of praise.
Resisting power, a shaggy head is shaken.
Authority welcomed by many and refused by few, he's aware of too much prestige in the world, too much certainty that botched term for presumption, too much love spiralling to mushy excesses like antibiotics losing influence when over prescribed.

Greatness dismissed, the bent sapling straightens.
Shuddering within shadows, dust blown and fatigued, wrinkled and sunburnt, stones are sucked to cheat thirst.
Evil refused snarls to a standstill, losing influence it's deprived of power, every swaggered moment a flying seed clutching its own destruction.
Losing resistance, eager for the last word, *Deceiver* departs, a rush of wind racing into nothingness, a ghost departing but ready to return.
Hoodwinked and befooled, while eager to destroy, he unwittingly becomes Purifier – all things opposing subtly strengthening.

IN TOUCH WITH THE ETERNAL

From crimson skies shoot Shining Ones – cosmic novelties juggled by *Grand Mystery*.
Cheered by food – *deity* dipped into wine and spread upon bread, thoughts are whispered not muttered in synagogue, temple, mosque or church.
Enigmas stifling comprehension, axioms absent from language, smatterings of the scarce greater than torrents of the understood.
Dependable spirituality never instant but slowly arriving, otherwise it overwhelms.
Hope Man is traveller – travellers advance in slow stages!

Staggering from isolation, hands dragging him forward, push him back,
    hunched shoulders wailing:
        "What does it all mean?"
        "Is it necessary?"
        "To what end, for what purpose?"
        "I should have remained a carpenter, vine dresser or potter."
        "Is it too late to commence something new?"
Or relieved, maybe he secretly smiles!
Some calamities impossible to endure unless we laugh at *God*, sneer at evil and contemplate *Creator* with humour as well as awe.
The moon has its phases, tides ebb and flow. Jaded and overwhelmed, so does he, sensitive natures always fragile.
Meanings and interpretations are craved, but at present,
    "The thimble is concealed."
    "I've hidden, you discover,"
    "I'll hide, you find me," 5.
And other playful messages hidden in praiseworthy bottles waiting to be found.
Careful wisdom games like, "hide and seek," old fashioned "hunt the slipper, wise play within play, secrets beyond secretiveness, mysteries resisting explanation enticing to higher things until puzzles click into pictures and cock-eyed parts lock together.

INTERMISSION:
PLEASE PAUSE IN RETROSPECT

Beyond endless skies of terrifying darkness, brightest stars and worlds lonely and austere, puppy heart of *Creator God* poises in wanton spontaneity.
Never taking *Itself* seriously – an eye for the ridiculous, a passion to invent, *Divinity* creates in playful intemperance, celebrated in loudest "Alleluias," every "Wow" and "Whoopee" surpassing solemn veneration – *"the laughter of the universe,"* gurgled Dante –
God's wink, scamper of hilarity, novelty and serendipity shouting: *"From the beginning before the earth came into being, I was the craftsman at his side delighting in him day after day **ever at play** in his presence, **at play everywhere in his world."***
"I God am your playmate," nodded Mechtild of Magdeburg – wisdom playing, us joining in.

It's playtime!

Eternal Love emptied of necessity, all times riotously free, playing games in rompish play with serious strategy.
Ordered imagination pretending *Itself* into frogs, flowers and necessary people, angels in cosmic dance rollicking among beauty never going anywhere.
No infernal destruction, obligation or compulsion but care-less play before earth began.
Mystery games, unwrinkled make-believe and magic in tiny secrets children have; mischievous inspiration and romping creativity celebrating magnificent absurdities.
In pleasurable kicks and buzzes like children leaping up and down while unwrapping Christmas presents … *"God creating man in order to be created by him,"* 6. games necessary to *Deity* as well as us. Why not? *"For the **foolishness of God** is wiser than men, and the weakness of God is stronger than men."*
Fancifully inventing, *Everlasting One* drenched in sensible fantasy and serious frivolity.
An immanence of childhood inquisitiveness, relaxed nonsense and playful paradox, awe and incredulity chasing all that can't be caught in youthful foolishness.
Absent from restrictions, eager for game play, *Eternal Child – Us in Him, Him in Us,* stomping from school in riotous freedom, blind fun and absent tediousness.
Clumsy Love, giddy, frisky and endearing, throwing stones at tin cans, talking to teddy bears, dragging sticks along railings, dribbling a ball down the street, running, jumping, visualising, romanticising and concocting enchantment identifying us closest to *Creator*.
A bustling wonderland crammed with children's make-believe and cherished secrets, gentle cruelty and innocent mischief always necessary to play.
"Life must be lived as play," laughed Plato.
Everyone needs to be taken out of themselves – precipitation into imaginary worlds, having fun wasting time, head-over-heels among spiritual immensities and holy accidents, a letting go and doing nothing in order to become something, our deepest feelings swapping law and obedience for the incredible.
Time standing still, responsibilities forgotten in metaphorical yanks of God's beard, a pinching of *His* ear, for if *God* can't become human and humans divine, both implode!

Part of the game being in playing with his children *he* hides *Himself*.

"The glory of God is to conceal a thing," noted knowledgeable Solomon, secrets always heaviest weights too carry.

In Blind-man's buff through wit reeking of complicities to a plot, *Deity* hides answers and solutions, games hurrying us along to the end in order to be finally found out!

No spectators, everyone participants daring much to win much.

No detentions of judgement but final surprise and laughter when gentle mischief melts into ridiculousness and childlike follies draw us closer to *Creator* in endless hide and seek, fun being in not knowing – **"Now you see, now you don't"** in conjuring tricks inciting search.

In light touches, *Creator* stooping in hiding, the amusement of the game being ignorance of its order for why continue if outcomes are known?

A teasing awareness of the forestalled and unanticipated, a hiddenness surpassing everything in efforts to surprise.

"Mysteries (games) *of the Kingdom,"* relished Galilee man, everyone participating in different guises and beliefs.

Less puzzles solved, more playful immediacy, every rule defying explanation, experiences not making sense, *Deity* keeping secrets just as we do – why not?

Nothing hoodwinking progress, everyone winning because *He* **lost**, and all we don't understand helping us to finally understand, so, *"If you can't partner me in play, don't have the impudence to question the rules. Just join in!"*

Joining in extends the game, everything choreographed from brightest star to smallest snail, *Creator* making first move, ourselves puzzling the second.

"I know something you don't know; just wait and see!" poking fun at our undeviating beliefs, mocking our prejudices, humouring our certainties, frolicking among our theology.

Juvenile grandeur poured into the incapable, everyone romping participators awaiting final solutions.

Without playful contradictions, jests of absurdity, entertaining secrets and games of mercy, the universe crashes into misery and ruin.

YEARNING FOR THE UNATTAINABLE

Puzzles set before us, the question remains, if *God* wields responsibility, why remain hidden?

If *he* playfully hides, he should politely appear.

But answers never come simply on a plate – it would spoil the game!

So much teasing, little revealing, God's hiding stopping us arrogantly imagining that we can prove his existence.

Playfully paradoxical, questions becomes answers, plunging doubts the most instructive and truths no longer believed as emancipating as those that do.

Unsettled by the inexplicable, with nothing left to say, acceptance is the only way of saying it.

Games played, thimbles hidden, everyone left to surmise, the inconclusive finally becoming the meaning – life's deepest truths, like heart, lungs and kidneys, only kept alive when carefully hidden.

"Hints and guesses," said Elliot, a hidden *Deity* carelessly giving itself away in
    red suns sinking into vast oceans,
    timeless stars in solemn beauty,
    surprise gusts of happiness and joy close to anguish,
    baby eyes where *He* passes without being seen,
    recovered memories of innocent events forgotten and innumerable crowded mysteries arousing longing and torment, everyone struggling to interpret things felt and seen.
Eternal Wonder constantly cheating in brief appearances and hasty withdrawals, contributing but never completely, telling little yet steering in hiddenness, our every glimpse half-revealing like tunes gone out of the head or dropping something that can't be found.
Feverishly seeking, hating obscurities, constantly questioning, plagued and baffled, we inch toward inspired impossibilities in romping games of "wait and see," "hide and seek," "thimble lost, thimble found:"
If life is a riotous game of "I've lost, you win," not knowing, our only comfort is playing "Let's pretend" until we finally know better.
Saved by hope not certainty, we are all left to cheerfully guess, gamble and play, God throwing the ball, ourselves dog-like chasing it.

SPLENDID DEPARTURE

His desert stay has ended.
Bundle of aroused nerves with nowhere to lay his head, hope lingers in spirit.
Fatigued but patient, he let's himself be led.
Like ourselves – pieces in a game, tales without endings; in hiding and seeking he presses toward the felt, sensed but not always understood, not the end of the story, just a pause, no hurry, the quest being arrival, the greatest virtue perseverance not attainment.
Triumph shot through with ambiguity, the wind covering footprints in the sand, *Wanderer* shoulders his bag and with quiet feet departs –the motion of the leaf indicating the flow of the air, God ahead of him but out of sight.

1. *Dostoesvky.*
2. *E. M. Forster.*
3. *Wordsworth.*
4. *Early Sufi mystic.*
5. *An idea from Charles Peguy.*
6. *Andre Gide.*

EPILOGUE

Since Jesus was born, and grew up in his full stature, and died, everything has continued to move forward *because Christ is not yet fully formed:* he has not yet gathered about him the last folds of his robe of flesh and of love ... The mystical Christ has not yet attained to his full growth; and therefore the same is true of the cosmic Christ. Both of these are simultaneously in the state of being and becoming; and it is from the prolongation of this process of becoming that all created activity ultimately springs. Christ is the end-point of the evolution, even the *natural* evolution of all beings; and therefore evolution is holy.

Hymn of the Universe.
Teilhard de Chardin.
(William Collins. 1961)

Printed in Great Britain
by Amazon